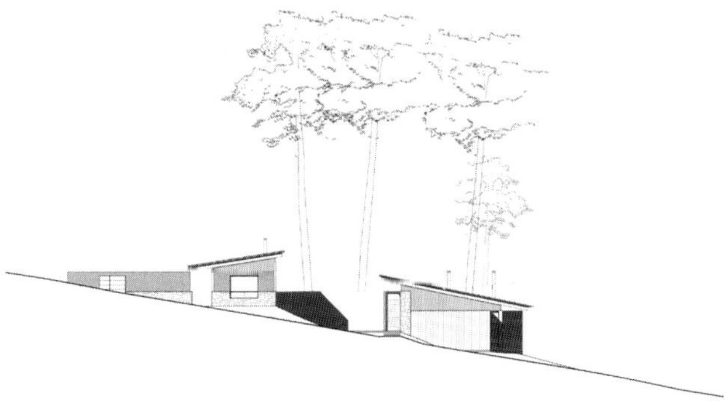

Editorial project:
© 2024 **booq** publishing, S.L.
c/ Domènech, 7-9, 2º 1ª
08012 Barcelona, Spain
T: +34 93 268 80 88
www.loftpublications.com

ISBN: 978 84 9936 629 6 [EN]
ISBN: 978 84 9936 619 7 [ES]

Editorial coordinator:
Claudia Martínez Alonso

Art director:
Mireia Casanovas Soley

Editor:
David Andreu Bach

Layout:
David Andreu Bach

Translation:
© booq publishing, S.L.

Printing in Spain

In the heart of our rapidly evolving world, where the transient and the ephemeral often overshadow the enduring and the substantial, "Wood: Cozy Interiors for Timeless Living Spaces" emerges as a beacon of warmth and sustainability. This book is not merely a collection; it is an odyssey through the tactile and timeless beauty of wood, showcasing the work of 27 distinguished architecture studios. Each project within these pages is a testament to the versatility and enduring appeal of wood, an element that has provided shelter and comfort to humanity through the ages. As we explore these spaces, we embark on a journey that transcends the mere aesthetic, delving into the essence of what it means to create environments that resonate with our deepest sense of home.

Wood, as a material, carries within it the whispers of the forest, the stories of growth and renewal. Its use in interior design is not only a choice of style but a commitment to sustainability and well-being. The projects featured in "Wood: Cozy Interiors for Timeless Living Spaces" illuminate the myriad ways in which architects and designers harness the natural warmth, resilience, and adaptability of wood to craft spaces that comfort and inspire. From the tactile pleasure of walking barefoot on a smooth wooden floor to the serene ambiance that wood-paneled walls can evoke, this book celebrates the material's unparalleled ability to create interiors that are both functional and inviting.

Moreover, this collection underscores the advantages of wood beyond its aesthetic appeal. Wood's inherent properties, such as its ability to regulate humidity and its excellent thermal insulation, contribute significantly to energy efficiency and environmental sustainability. In an era where the conversation around building materials is increasingly dominated by concerns over carbon footprints and environmental impact, the projects within these pages stand as exemplars of how thoughtful use of wood can lead to living spaces that are not only beautiful but also kind to our planet.

"Wood: Cozy Interiors for Timeless Living Spaces" is more than a book; it is an invitation to reimagine the spaces we inhabit and the materials we use to shape them. It invites readers, whether architects, designers, or simply lovers of timeless interiors, to explore the profound connection between the natural world and our living spaces. Through its pages, we are reminded of the enduring legacy of wood in architecture and interior design, and of the beauty and sustainability that are possible when we choose materials with care and intention. This book is a tribute to the material that has served as the backbone of our shelters and homes for centuries, and a guide for those seeking to create spaces that marry tradition with innovation, and sustainability with style.

Im Herzen unserer sich schnell entwickelnden Welt, in der das Vergängliche und das Flüchtige oft das Beständige und Substanzielle überschatten, erhebt sich „Holz: Gemütliche Innenräume für zeitlose Wohnräume" als Leuchtfeuer von Wärme und Nachhaltigkeit. Dieses Buch ist nicht bloß eine Sammlung; es ist eine Odyssee durch die haptische und zeitlose Schönheit von Holz, das die Arbeit von 27 renommierten Architekturbüros präsentiert. Jedes Projekt in diesen Seiten ist ein Zeugnis für die Vielseitigkeit und die bleibende Anziehungskraft von Holz, einem Element, das den Menschen im Laufe der Jahrhunderte Schutz und Komfort geboten hat. Während wir diese Räume erkunden, begeben wir uns auf eine Reise, die über das bloß Ästhetische hinausgeht und in die Essenz dessen eintaucht, was es bedeutet, Umgebungen zu schaffen, die mit unserem tiefsten Gefühl von Zuhause in Resonanz stehen.

Holz trägt als Material in sich die Flüstern des Waldes, die Geschichten des Wachstums und der Erneuerung. Sein Einsatz in der Innenarchitektur ist nicht nur eine Stilwahl, sondern ein Bekenntnis zur Nachhaltigkeit und zum Wohlbefinden. Die in „Holz: Gemütliche Innenräume für zeitlose Wohnräume" vorgestellten Projekte beleuchten die vielfältigen Möglichkeiten, wie Architekten und Designer die natürliche Wärme, Belastbarkeit und Anpassungsfähigkeit von Holz nutzen, um Räume zu gestalten, die trösten und inspirieren. Vom haptischen Vergnügen, barfuß auf einem glatten Holzboden zu gehen, bis zur ruhigen Atmosphäre, die holzvertäfelte Wände hervorrufen können, feiert dieses Buch die beispiellose Fähigkeit des Materials, Innenräume zu schaffen, die sowohl funktional als auch einladend sind.

Darüber hinaus unterstreicht diese Sammlung die Vorteile von Holz jenseits seiner ästhetischen Anziehungskraft. Die inhärenten Eigenschaften von Holz, wie seine Fähigkeit, Feuchtigkeit zu regulieren, und seine ausgezeichnete thermische Isolierung, tragen erheblich zur Energieeffizienz und Umweltschonung bei. In einer Ära, in der die Diskussion über Baustoffe zunehmend von Bedenken hinsichtlich des CO2-Fußabdrucks und der Umweltauswirkungen dominiert wird, stehen die Projekte in diesen Seiten als Beispiele dafür, wie der durchdachte Einsatz von Holz zu Wohnräumen führen kann, die nicht nur schön, sondern auch umweltfreundlich sind.

„Holz: Gemütliche Innenräume für zeitlose Wohnräume" ist mehr als ein Buch; es ist eine Einladung, die Räume, die wir bewohnen, und die Materialien, die wir verwenden, neu zu denken. Es lädt die Leser, sei es Architekten, Designer oder einfach nur Liebhaber zeitloser Innenräume, ein, die tiefe Verbindung zwischen der natürlichen Welt und unseren Lebensräumen zu erkunden. Durch seine Seiten werden wir an das bleibende Erbe von Holz in Architektur und Innenarchitektur erinnert und an die Schönheit und Nachhaltigkeit, die möglich sind, wenn wir Materialien mit Sorgfalt und Absicht wählen. Dieses Buch ist eine Hommage an das Material, das seit Jahrhunderten als Rückgrat unserer Schutzhütten und Häuser dient, und ein Leitfaden für diejenigen, die Räume schaffen wollen, die Tradition mit Innovation und Nachhaltigkeit mit Stil verbinden.

Au cœur de notre monde en évolution rapide, où le transitoire et l'éphémère obscurcissent souvent le durable et le substantiel, « Wood: Cozy Interiors for Timeless Living Spaces » émerge comme un phare de chaleur et de durabilité. Ce livre n'est pas simplement une collection ; c'est une odyssée à travers la beauté tactile et intemporelle du bois, mettant en valeur le travail de 27 studios d'architecture distingués. Chaque projet dans ces pages est un témoignage de la polyvalence et de l'attrait durable du bois, un élément qui a fourni abri et confort à l'humanité à travers les âges. En explorant ces espaces, nous embarquons pour un voyage qui transcende le simple esthétique, en plongeant dans l'essence de ce que cela signifie de créer des environnements qui résonnent avec notre sens le plus profond du foyer.

Le bois, en tant que matériau, porte en lui les murmures de la forêt, les histoires de croissance et de renouveau. Son utilisation dans la conception intérieure n'est pas seulement un choix de style mais un engagement envers la durabilité et le bien-être. Les projets présentés dans « Wood: Cozy Interiors for Timeless Living Spaces » illuminent les innombrables façons dont les architectes et les designers exploitent la chaleur naturelle, la résilience et l'adaptabilité du bois pour créer des espaces qui réconfortent et inspirent. Du plaisir tactile de marcher pieds nus sur un sol en bois lisse à l'ambiance sereine que peuvent évoquer les murs lambrissés en bois, ce livre célèbre la capacité inégalée du matériau à créer des intérieurs à la fois fonctionnels et accueillants.

De plus, cette collection souligne les avantages du bois au-delà de son attrait esthétique. Les propriétés inhérentes du bois, telles que sa capacité à réguler l'humidité et son excellente isolation thermique, contribuent de manière significative à l'efficacité énergétique et à la durabilité environnementale. À une époque où la conversation sur les matériaux de construction est de plus en plus dominée par des préoccupations concernant les empreintes carbone et l'impact environnemental, les projets présentés dans ces pages sont des exemples de l'utilisation réfléchie du bois qui peut conduire à des espaces de vie non seulement beaux mais aussi respectueux de notre planète.

« Wood: Cozy Interiors for Timeless Living Spaces » est plus qu'un livre ; c'est une invitation à réimaginer les espaces que nous habitons et les matériaux que nous utilisons pour les façonner. Il invite les lecteurs, qu'ils soient architectes, designers, ou simplement amateurs d'intérieurs intemporels, à explorer la profonde connexion entre le monde naturel et nos espaces de vie. À travers ses pages, nous sommes rappelés de l'héritage durable du bois dans l'architecture et la conception intérieure, ainsi que de la beauté et de la durabilité qui sont possibles lorsque nous choisissons des matériaux avec soin et intention. Ce livre est un hommage au matériau qui a servi de pilier à nos abris et maisons depuis des siècles, et un guide pour ceux qui cherchent à créer des espaces qui marient tradition et innovation, et durabilité et style.

En el corazón de nuestro mundo, que evoluciona rápidamente, donde lo transitorio y efímero a menudo eclipsa lo duradero y sustancial, emerge «Madera: Interiores acogedores» como un faro de calidez y sostenibilidad. Este libro no es simplemente una colección; es una odisea a través de la belleza táctil y atemporal de la madera, mostrando el trabajo de 27 distinguidos estudios de arquitectura. Cada proyecto dentro de estas páginas es un testimonio de la versatilidad y el atractivo perdurable de la madera, un elemento que ha proporcionado refugio y confort a la humanidad a través de las edades. A medida que exploramos estos espacios, nos embarcamos en un viaje que trasciende lo meramente estético, adentrándonos en la esencia de lo que significa crear ambientes que resuenen con nuestro sentido más profundo de hogar.

La madera, como material, lleva dentro de sí los susurros del bosque, las historias de crecimiento y renovación. Su uso en el diseño interior no es solo una elección de estilo, sino un compromiso con la ecología y el bienestar. Los proyectos presentados en este precioso volumen iluminan las innumerables maneras en que arquitectos y diseñadores aprovechan el calor natural, la resiliencia y la adaptabilidad de la madera para crear espacios que confortan e inspiran. Desde el placer táctil de caminar descalzo sobre un suave suelo de madera hasta el ambiente sereno que pueden evocar las paredes revestidas, este libro celebra la capacidad incomparable del material para crear interiores que son tanto funcionales como acogedores.

Además, esta colección subraya las ventajas de la madera más allá de su atractivo estético. Las propiedades inherentes de la madera, como su capacidad para regular la humedad y su excelente aislamiento térmico, contribuyen significativamente a la eficiencia energética y la sostenibilidad ambiental. En una era donde la conversación en torno a los materiales de construcción está cada vez más dominada por preocupaciones sobre huellas de carbono e impacto ambiental, los proyectos dentro de estas páginas se erigen como ejemplos de cómo el uso reflexivo de la madera puede conducir a espacios de vida que no solo son hermosos, sino también amables con nuestro planeta.

«Madera: Interiores Acogedores» es más que un libro; es una invitación a reimaginar los espacios que habitamos y los materiales que usamos para darles forma. Invita a los lectores, ya sean arquitectos, diseñadores o simplemente amantes de interiores atemporales, a explorar la profunda conexión entre el mundo natural y nuestros espacios de vida. A través de sus páginas, se nos recuerda el legado perdurable de la madera en la arquitectura y el diseño de interiores, y de la belleza que son posibles cuando elegimos materiales con cuidado e intención. Este libro es un tributo al material que ha servido como la columna vertebral de nuestros refugios y hogares durante siglos, y una guía para aquellos que buscan crear espacios que unan la tradición con la innovación, y la sostenibilidad con el estilo.

Quality of space emerges when vision, creativity, craftsmanship and decisiveness meet. Achterbosch Architecten uses a critical attitude, resulting in a portfolio of original, innovative and often experimental designs. Years of experience and a deep love for nature intertwine seamlessly in locally tailored solutions in every design to ensure the right balance between aesthetics and sustainability.
Achterbosch Architecten engages in regional projects as well as projects all over the world. Within major and integral design tasks, we are convinced that gathering a wide scope of experience and intellect is necessary. For this leads to professionalism and enhances the quality of architecture and urbanism service.
In addition, we share our insights into the latest developments in the field of circular and bio-based materials and the positive effects of these building materials on the human psyche.

Die Qualität des Raumes entsteht, wenn Vision, Kreativität, Handwerk und Entscheidung zusammenkommen. Achterbosch Architecten verwendet eine kritische Haltung, was zu einer Portfolio von originellen, innovativen und oft experimentellen Designs führt. Jahre der Erfahrung und eine tiefe Liebe zur Natur verschmelzen nahtlos zu lokal angepassten Lösungen in jedem Design, um das richtige Gleichgewicht zwischen Ästhetik und Nachhaltigkeit zu gewährleisten.
Achterbosch Architecten ist an regionalen und weltweiten Projekten beteiligt. Wir sind der Überzeugung, dass bei den wichtigsten und umfassendsten Designaufgaben ein breites Spektrum an Erfahrung und Intellekt zusammengeführt werden muss, da dies zu Professionalität führt und die Qualität des Architektur- und Städtebauservice verbessert.
Darüber hinaus teilen wir unser Wissen über die neuesten Entwicklungen im Bereich der zirkulären und bio-basierten Materialien und die positiven Auswirkungen dieser Baustoffe auf die menschliche Psyche.

La qualité de l'espace émerge lorsque la vision, la créativité, l'artisanat et la décision se rejoignent. Achterbosch Architecten adopte une attitude critique, ce qui se traduit par un portefeuille de conceptions originales, innovantes et souvent expérimentales. Des années d'expérience et un profond amour de la nature s'entremêlent parfaitement dans des solutions adaptées localement dans chaque conception pour garantir le bon équilibre entre esthétique et durabilité.
Achterbosch Architecten participe à des projets régionaux et mondiaux. Nous sommes convaincus que, dans les tâches de conception les plus importantes et les plus intégrales, il est nécessaire de réunir une vaste expérience et une intellect parce que cela conduit à la professionnalité et améliore la qualité du service d'architecture et d'urbanisme.
De plus, nous partageons nos connaissances sur les dernières avancées dans le domaine des matériaux circulaires et biobasés et les effets positifs de ces matériaux de construction sur la psyché humaine.

La calidad del espacio surge cuando confluyen visión, creatividad, artesanía y decisión. Achterbosch Architecten utiliza una actitud crítica, lo que da como resultado una cartera de diseños originales, innovadores y a menudo experimentales. Años de experiencia y un profundo amor por la naturaleza se entrelazan a la perfección en soluciones adaptadas localmente en cada diseño para garantizar el equilibrio adecuado entre estética y sostenibilidad.
Achterbosch Architecten participa en proyectos regionales y de todo el mundo. Estamos convencidos de que, en las tareas de diseño más importantes e integrales, es necesario reunir una amplia experiencia e intelecto porque esto conduce a la profesionalidad y mejora la calidad del servicio de arquitectura y urbanismo.
Además, compartimos nuestros conocimientos sobre los últimos avances en el campo de los materiales circulares y de base biológica y los efectos positivos de estos materiales de construcción en la psique humana.

Achterbosch Architecten

www.achterboscharchitecten.nl

Hans Achterbosch
Liang Wei

© Laurens Aaij

Energy Knowledge Center

Meijie Mountain Hotspring Resort

This circular office is a meeting place and platform for innovation in today's energy issues. The Energy Knowledge Center is located on a former landfill site and is placed on 108 individually adjustable columns. Should the soil on the ground level start to move or subside, the columns are individually adjustable to prevent damage to the building. To keep these columns accessible, the removable building is placed 1.5 meters above ground level. The building is completely self-sufficient in terms of energy management, including the use of solar panels and heat pumps. Gases emitted from the former garbage dump inside the hill are used for heating. This building shows in a smart and effective way how land can be re-used, even in this former polluted environment.

Dieses kreisförmige Büro ist ein Treffpunkt und eine Plattform für Innovationen in aktuellen Energiefragen. Das Zentrum für Energiewissen befindet sich auf einer alten Mülldeponie und ruht auf 108 einzeln verstellbaren Säulen. Sollte der Boden zu bewegen oder zu sinken beginnen, können die Säulen einzeln eingestellt werden, um Schäden am Gebäude zu vermeiden. Damit diese Säulen zugänglich sind, ist das abbaubare Gebäude 1,5 m über dem Bodenniveau platziert. Das Gebäude ist in Bezug auf das Energiemanagement vollständig autark, einschließlich der Verwendung von Solarpaneelen und Wärmepumpen. Die Gase, die aus der alten Mülldeponie im Inneren des Hügels emittiert werden, werden zur Beheizung genutzt. Dieses Gebäude zeigt intelligent und effektiv, wie der Boden wiederverwendet werden kann, selbst in dieser alten kontaminierten Umgebung.

Ce bureau circulaire est un lieu de rencontre et une plateforme pour l'innovation dans les problèmes énergétiques actuels. Le Centre de Connaissance de l'Énergie est situé sur un ancien dépotoir et repose sur 108 colonnes réglables individuellement. En cas de mouvement ou d'affaissement du sol, les colonnes peuvent être ajustées individuellement pour éviter d'endommager le bâtiment. Pour que ces colonnes soient accessibles, le bâtiment démontable est situé à 1,5 mètre au-dessus du niveau du sol. Le bâtiment est entièrement autonome en termes de gestion énergétique, y compris l'utilisation de panneaux solaires et de pompes à chaleur. Les gaz émis par l'ancienne décharge de déchets à l'intérieur de la colline sont utilisés pour le chauffage. Ce bâtiment montre de manière intelligente et efficace comment le sol peut être réutilisé, même dans cet ancien environnement contaminé.

Esta oficina circular es un lugar de encuentro y una plataforma para la innovación en los problemas energéticos actuales. El Centro del Conocimiento de la Energía está situado en un antiguo vertedero y se asienta sobre 108 columnas ajustables individualmente. En caso de que el suelo empiece a moverse o a hundirse, las columnas se pueden ajustar individualmente para evitar daños al edificio. Para que estas columnas sean accesibles, el edificio desmontable está situado a 1,5 m por encima del nivel del suelo. El edificio es completamente autosuficiente en términos de gestión energética, incluido el uso de paneles solares y bombas de calor. Los gases emitidos por el antiguo vertedero de basura del interior de la colina se utilizan para la calefacción. Este edificio muestra de forma inteligente y eficaz cómo se puede reutilizar el suelo, incluso en este antiguo entorno contaminado.

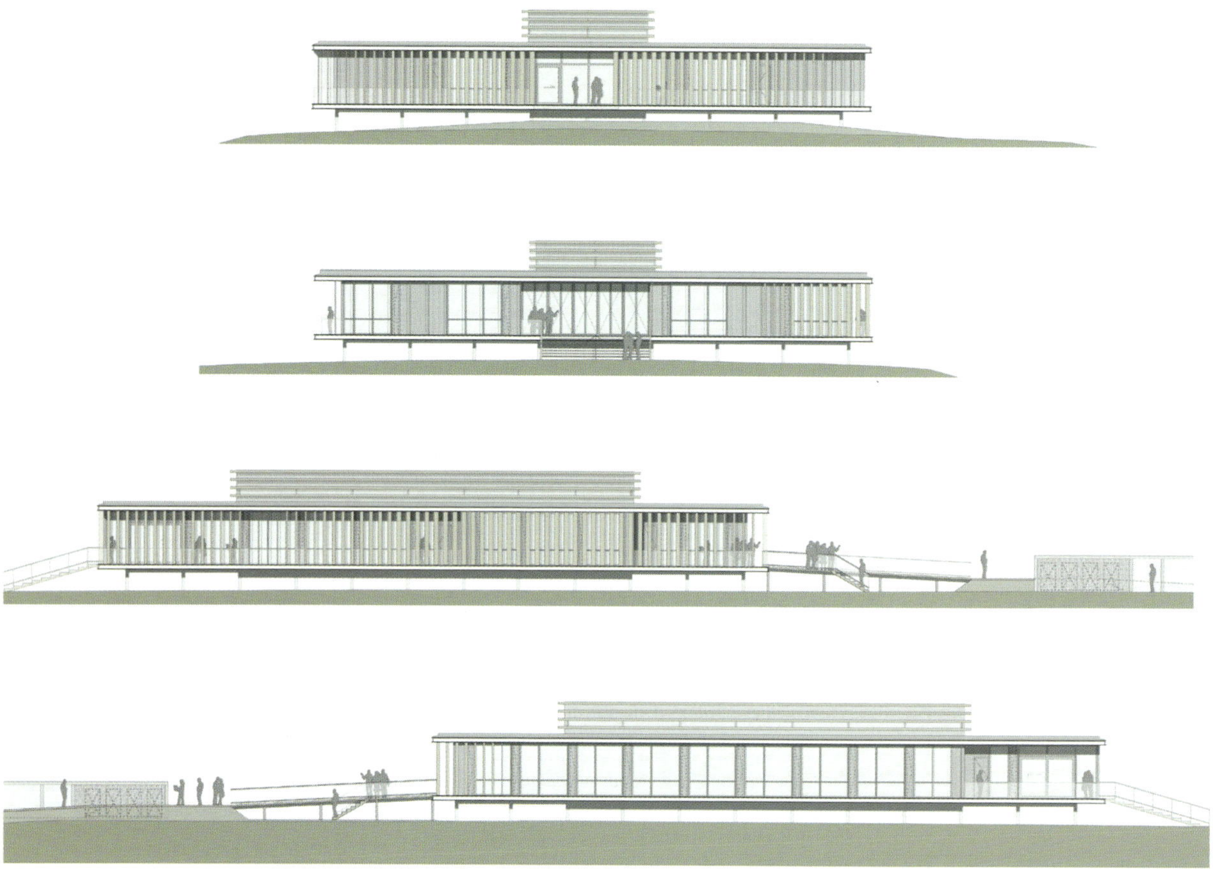

Facades

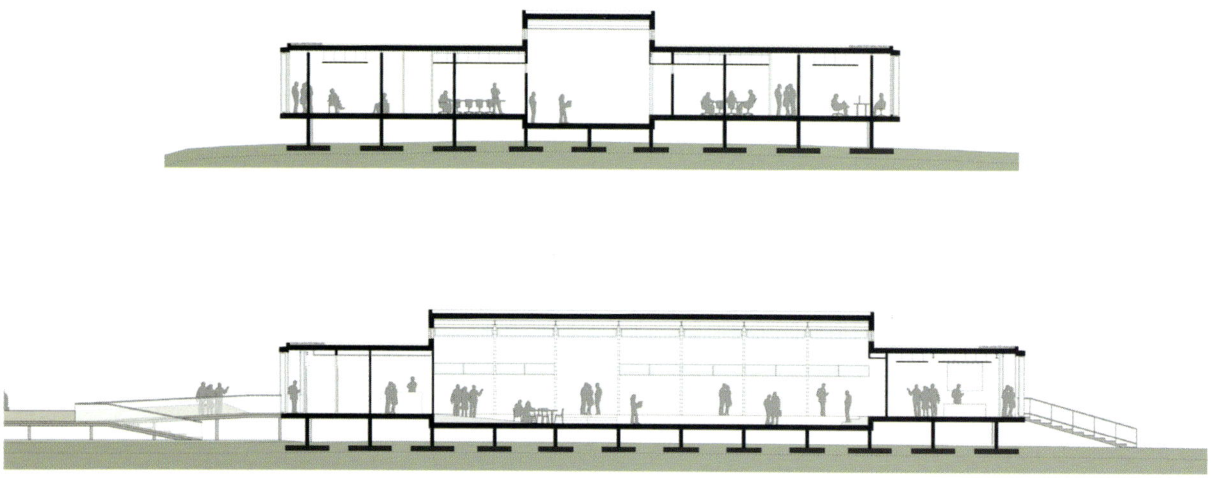

Sections

Liyang, China // Photos © Anna de Leeuw

This resort is hidden in a beautiful forest between Tianmu Lake and Nanshan Bamboo. It combines four ecological elements: forest, tree houses, hot springs and mountains. The resort is suitable for recreational tourism as well as for business gatherings. A total of 31 tree houses have been cleverly set up and have been constructed with natural materials. All the tree houses have been designed to fully meet the wishes of the guests and have a fresh, natural and cozy appearance. All details including furniture and lighting are chosen by Achterbosch Architecten. The resort has pools of hot springs. The spring pools are independent from each other to ensure privacy. The Meijie Mountain Hotspring Resort reveals the concept of sustainable design: originality, ingeniousness, transparency, delicacy.

Diese Anlage ist in einem wunderschönen Wald zwischen dem Tianmu-See und Nanshan Bamboo versteckt. Sie kombiniert vier ökologische Elemente: Wald, Baumhäuser, Thermalquellen und Berge. Die Anlage eignet sich sowohl für Erholungstourismus als auch für Geschäftstreffen. Insgesamt wurden 31 Baumhäuser einfallsreich installiert und aus Naturmaterialien gebaut. Alle Baumhäuser wurden so konzipiert, dass sie die Wünsche der Gäste vollständig erfüllen und ein frisches, natürliches und einladendes Ambiente bieten. Alle Details, einschließlich Möbel und Beleuchtung, wurden von Achterbosch Architecten ausgewählt. Die Anlage verfügt über Thermalpools. Die Quellenpools sind voneinander unabhängig, um die Privatsphäre zu gewährleisten. Das Meijie Mountain Hotspring Resort offenbart das Konzept nachhaltigen Designs: Originalität, Einfallsreichtum, Transparenz, Feinheit.

Ce complexe est caché dans une belle forêt entre le lac Tianmu et le bambou de Nanshan. Il combine quatre éléments écologiques : la forêt, les maisons dans les arbres, les sources chaudes et les montagnes. Le complexe est adapté aussi bien au tourisme récréatif qu'aux réunions d'affaires. Un total de 31 maisons dans les arbres ont été ingénieusement installées et construites avec des matériaux naturels. Toutes les maisons dans les arbres ont été conçues pour répondre pleinement aux souhaits des clients et ont un aspect frais, naturel et accueillant. Tous les détails, y compris les meubles et l'éclairage, ont été choisis par Achterbosch Architecten. Le complexe dispose de piscines thermales. Les piscines de source sont indépendantes les unes des autres pour garantir l'intimité. Le Meijie Mountain Hotspring Resort révèle le concept de design durable : originalité, ingéniosité, transparence, délicatesse.

Este complejo está escondido en un hermoso bosque entre el lago Tianmu y Nanshan Bamboo. Combina cuatro elementos ecológicos: bosque, casas en los árboles, aguas termales y montañas. El complejo es adecuado tanto para el turismo recreativo como para reuniones de negocios. Un total de 31 casas en los árboles han sido ingeniosamente instaladas y construidas con materiales naturales. Todas las casas en los árboles se han diseñado para satisfacer plenamente los deseos de los huéspedes y tienen un aspecto fresco, natural y acogedor. Todos los detalles, incluidos los muebles y la iluminación, han sido elegidos por Achterbosch Architecten. El complejo cuenta con piscinas de aguas termales. Las piscinas de manantiales son independientes entre sí para garantizar la privacidad. El Meijie Mountain Hotspring Resort revela el concepto de diseño sostenible: originalidad, ingenio, transparencia, delicadeza.

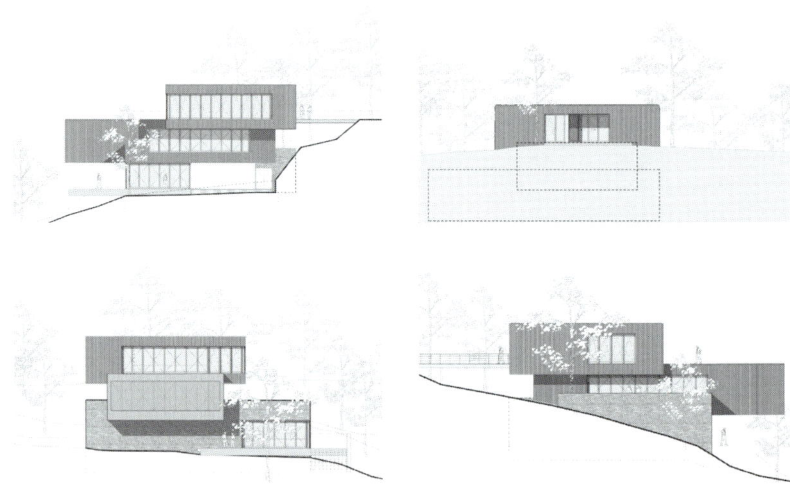

Club House elevations

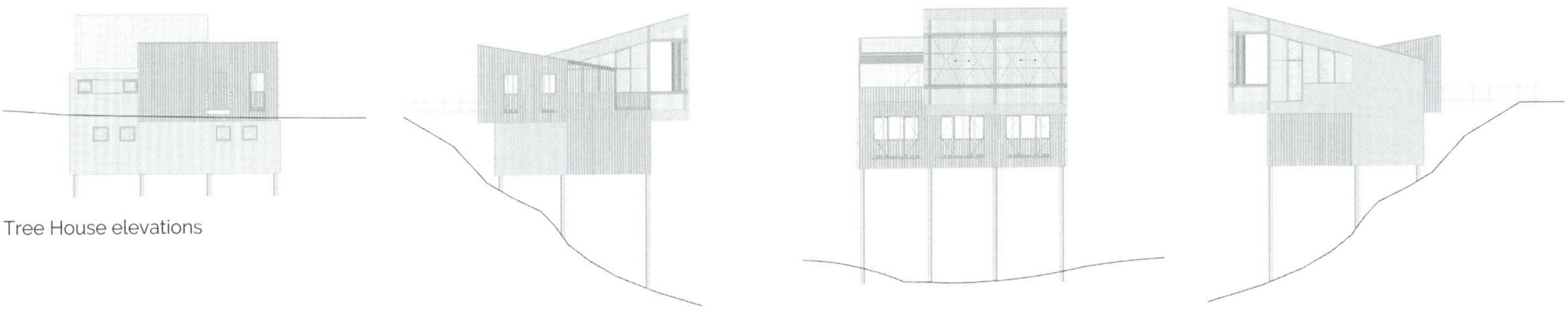

Tree House elevations

Founded in 2004 by Robert Kastelic and Kelly Buffey, Akb Architects is an internationally renowned, Toronto-based residential architecture studio dedicated to the practice and art of building. Akb's design process prioritizes a clarity of vision, attention to detail, and a rigorous commitment to conceptual intent. The prodigious quality of their work is a result of Robert and Kelly's synthesis of architectural, interior and technical design; a comprehensive strategy results in buildings of exceptional resolution and an uncommon level of refinement. A unified and holistic approach to interior and exterior space merges building and landscape into a seamless experience. Elements of volume, light, proportion and materiality are orchestrated to resonate and respond to each project's unique site, context and program. Compelling in their tranquility and quiet simplicity, the resulting buildings are warmly engaging, elegant and functional. Akb recognizes the importance of a collaborative process in maintaining an open dialogue with their clients, ensuring all needs and desires are met. Meticulous research, precedent studies and the deployment of current sustainability strategies enable the studio to fuse the practical and the abstract in an architecture that is creative, inspired and enduring.

Akb Architects wurde 2004 von Robert Kastelic und Kelly Buffey gegründet und ist ein international renommiertes Architekturbüro mit Sitz in Toronto, das sich der Praxis und Kunst des Bauens widmet. Der Entwurfsprozess von Akb legt den Schwerpunkt auf eine klare Vision, die Liebe zum Detail und die konsequente Umsetzung der konzeptionellen Absicht. Die herausragende Qualität ihrer Arbeit ist das Ergebnis von Robert und Kellys Synthese von Architektur, Inneneinrichtung und technischem Design. Eine umfassende Strategie führt zu Gebäuden von außergewöhnlicher Auflösung und einem ungewöhnlichen Maß an Raffinesse. Ein einheitlicher und ganzheitlicher Ansatz für den Innen- und Außenraum lässt Gebäude und Landschaft zu einem nahtlosen Erlebnis verschmelzen. Elemente wie Volumen, Licht, Proportionen und Materialität werden so inszeniert, dass sie auf den einzigartigen Standort, den Kontext und das Programm eines jeden Projekts abgestimmt sind. Die daraus resultierenden Gebäude bestechen durch ihre Ruhe und stille Einfachheit und sind warmherzig, elegant und funktional. Akb ist sich der Bedeutung eines gemeinschaftlichen Prozesses bewusst und pflegt einen offenen Dialog mit seinen Kunden, um sicherzustellen, dass alle Bedürfnisse und Wünsche erfüllt werden. Sorgfältige Recherchen, Präzedenzfallstudien und der Einsatz aktueller Nachhaltigkeitsstrategien ermöglichen es dem Studio, das Praktische und das Abstrakte in einer Architektur zu vereinen, die kreativ, inspiriert und dauerhaft ist.

Fondé en 2004 par Robert Kastelic et Kelly Buffey, Akb Architects est un studio d'architecture résidentielle de renommée internationale, basé à Toronto, qui se consacre à la pratique et à l'art de la construction. Le processus de conception d'Akb Architects donne la priorité à la clarté de la vision, à l'attention portée aux détails et à un engagement rigoureux envers l'intention conceptuelle. La qualité prodigieuse de leur travail est le résultat de la synthèse de Robert et Kelly entre l'architecture, l'intérieur et la conception technique ; une stratégie globale aboutit à des bâtiments d'une résolution exceptionnelle et d'un niveau de raffinement peu commun. Une approche unifiée et holistique de l'espace intérieur et extérieur fusionne le bâtiment et le paysage en une expérience homogène. Les éléments de volume, de lumière, de proportion et de matérialité sont orchestrés pour répondre au site, au contexte et au programme de chaque projet. Akb reconnaît l'importance d'un processus de collaboration en maintenant un dialogue ouvert avec ses clients, en s'assurant que tous les besoins et désirs sont satisfaits. Une recherche méticuleuse, des études de précédents et le déploiement de stratégies de durabilité actuelles permettent au studio de fusionner le pratique et l'abstrait dans une architecture créative, inspirée et durable.

Fundado en 2004 por Robert Kastelic y Kelly Buffey, Akb Architects es un estudio de arquitectura residencial de renombre internacional con sede en Toronto dedicado a la construcción. El proceso de diseño de Akb prioriza la claridad de visión, la atención al detalle y un compromiso con la intención conceptual. La calidad de su trabajo es el resultado de la síntesis de diseño arquitectónico, interior y técnico de Robert y Kelly; una estrategia integral que da como resultado edificios de excepcional resolución y un gran nivel de refinamiento. Un enfoque unificado y global del espacio interior y exterior fusiona el edificio y el paisaje en una experiencia sin fisuras. Los elementos de volumen, luz, proporción y materialidad se orquestan para que resuenen y respondan al emplazamiento, contexto y programa únicos de cada proyecto. Akb reconoce la importancia de un proceso de colaboración para mantener un diálogo abierto con sus clientes, garantizando que se satisfagan todas las necesidades y deseos. La investigación meticulosa, los estudios de precedentes y el despliegue de estrategias de sostenibilidad actuales permiten al estudio fusionar lo práctico y lo abstracto en una arquitectura creativa, inspirada y duradera.

Akb Architects

www.akb.ca

Robert Kastelic
Kelly Buffey

Muskoka Cottage

Muskoka, Ontario, Canada // Photos © Shai Gil, Lauren Miller

This multi-generational family cottage is clad in rough-sawn cedar boards and western red cedar shakes to blend seamlessly with the northern Ontario terrain of windswept trees and Pre-Cambrian bedrock. The 7,500-square-foot residence is comprised of three interconnected volumes, crafting an interior characterized by both cozy spaces and open rooms, each providing spectacular views of a freshwater lake. The interior finishes emphasize the elemental, with bespoke concrete vanities and kitchen cabinetry discreetly integrated into the wood wall boards and aligned flush with the island's granite countertop. Soft furnishings, selected by Ashley Botten Design, and area rugs in neutral tones add warmth to the architectural interplay between rustic charm and finely crafted minimalism.
Siting the main volume on a naturally sloped elevation allowed for a lower level with a walk-out. A cedar sauna, fitness room, and recreation room are steps away from pathways leading to the boathouse and shoreline.

Diese multigenerationale Familienhütte, verkleidet mit gesägten Zedernbrettern und westlichen roten Zedernschindeln, verschmilzt mit der Landschaft im Norden von Ontario, wo Bäume vom Wind gepeitscht werden und präkambrischer Mutterfels liegt.
Die 697 m² große Residenz besteht aus drei miteinander verbundenen Volumen, die ein gemütliches Interieur und Zimmer mit spektakulärem Blick auf einen Süßwassersee bilden. Die Innenausstattung konzentriert sich auf das Elementare, mit maßgefertigten Betonwaschtischen und Küchenschränken, die so gestaltet sind, dass sie in die Wandverkleidungen übergehen und bündig mit der Granit-Arbeitsplatte der Insel abschließen. Von Ashley Botten Design ausgewählte Möbel und Teppiche in neutralen Tönen sorgen für Wärme, rustikalen Charme und minimalistische Handwerkskunst.
Die Platzierung des Hauptvolumens auf einer natürlichen Anhöhe ermöglichte ein unteres Niveau mit Ausgang. Eine Sauna aus Zedernholz, ein Fitnessraum und ein Spielzimmer befinden sich nur wenige Schritte von den Pfaden entfernt, die zum Bootssteg und zum Ufer führen.

Cabine Muskoka, cette cabane familiale multigénérationnelle revêtue de planches de cedre sciees et de tuiles de cèdre rouge occidental se fond avec le paysage du nord de l'Ontario, où les arbres sont balayés par le vent et la roche mère précambrienne.
La résidence de 697 mètres carrés comprend trois volumes interconnectés qui forment un intérieur de espaces accueillants et de chambres ouvertes avec des vues spectaculaires sur un lac d'eau douce. Les finitions intérieures se concentrent sur l'élémentaire, avec des vanités en béton sur mesure et des armoires de cuisine conçues pour se fondre dans les planches murales et courir à ras avec le comptoir en granit de l'îlot. Le mobilier, sélectionné par Ashley Botten Design, et les tapis dans des tons neutres ajoutent de la chaleur à l'interaction architecturale entre le charme rustique et l'artisanat minimaliste. Placer le volume principal sur une élévation naturelle a permis un niveau inférieur avec sortie. Un sauna en cèdre, une salle de fitness et une salle de jeux sont à quelques pas des sentiers menant à l'embarcadère et au rivage.

Esta cabaña familiar multigeneracional, revestida con tablas de cedro aserrado y tejas de cedro rojo occidental, se fusiona con el terreno del norte de Ontario de árboles azotados por el viento y roca madre precámbrica. La residencia, de 697 m² comprende tres volúmenes interconectados que forman un interior de espacios acogedores y habitaciones abiertas con vistas espectaculares a un lago de agua dulce. Los acabados interiores se centran en lo elemental, con vanidades de concreto hechas a medida y gabinetes de cocina hechos para fusionarse con las tablas de pared y correr enrasados con la encimera de granito de la isla. El mobiliario, seleccionado por Ashley Botten Design, y las alfombras en tonos neutros añaden calidez a la interacción arquitectónica entre el encanto rústico y el minimalismo de la artesanía.. Situar el volumen principal en una elevación natural permitió un nivel inferior con salida. Una sauna de cedro, una sala de fitness y una sala de recreo están a pasos de los senderos que conducen al embarcadero y la orilla.

Altamarea, an office established in 2015 by architect Gonzalo Herreros and engineer Matias Quinlan, is primarily characterized by its comprehensive development of housing projects and investments for the coastal area of Chile. We develop architecture that suits the location, recognizing the climatic conditions and their variations throughout the year. We build projects with simple materials of local origin, achieving great construction and architectural results.
Based on our beach life experience, we create living experiences focused on energy efficiency, light utilization, and long-lasting durability, key concepts in the development of our projects. Nowadays, Altamarea is involved in residential and commercial areas. In recent years, we have been working on hotel and commerce projects, aiming to provide an architectural image to our surroundings.

Altamarea ist ein Büro, das im Jahr 2015 vom Architekten Gonzalo Herreros und dem Ingenieur Matias Quinlan gegründet wurde. Es ist hauptsächlich auf die umfassende Entwicklung von Wohnprojekten und Investitionen an der chilenischen Küste spezialisiert. Wir entwickeln eine dem Ort angemessene Architektur, indem wir die klimatischen Bedingungen und ihre Veränderungen im Laufe des Jahres berücksichtigen. Wir bauen Projekte mit einfachen Materialien aus lokaler Herkunft, die zu großartigen Bauelementen und architektonischen Ergebnissen führen.
Basierend auf unserer Lebenserfahrung am Strand schaffen wir für unsere Kunden Lebenserfahrungen, die sich auf Energieeffizienz, Lichtnutzung und Langzeitbeständigkeit konzentrieren, Schlüsselkonzepte in der Entwicklung unserer Projekte. Heutzutage ist Altamarea im Wohn- und Gewerbebereich tätig. In den letzten Jahren haben wir an der Entwicklung von Hotel- und Handelsprojekten gearbeitet, um durch unseren Vorschlag ein architektonisches Bild unserer Umgebung zu vermitteln.

Altamarea est un bureau créé en 2015 par l'architecte Gonzalo Herreros et l'ingénieur Matias Quinlan, se distinguant principalement par le développement intégral de projets résidentiels et d'investissements pour la région côtière du Chili. L'architecture développée est en harmonie avec le lieu, reconnaissant les conditions climatiques et leurs variations tout au long de l'année. Les projets sont construits avec des matériaux simples d'origine locale, fournissant d'excellents résultats constructifs et architecturaux.
Forts de notre expérience de vie à la plage, nous créons des expériences de vie axées sur l'efficacité énergétique, l'utilisation optimale de la lumière et la durabilité, des concepts clés dans le développement de nos projets. Aujourd'hui, Altamarea s'engage dans le domaine résidentiel et commercial, travaillant également sur des projets hôteliers et commerciaux pour donner une identité architecturale à notre environnement.

Altamarea es una oficina creada el año 2015 por el arquitecto Gonzalo Herreros y el ingeniero Matias Quinlan. Se ha caracterizado principalmente por el desarrollo integral de proyectos de vivienda e inversiones para la zona costera de Chile. Desarrollamos una arquitectura acorde al lugar reconociendo las condiciones climáticas y sus variables a lo largo del año. Construimos proyectos con materiales sencillos de origen local, con grandes resultados constructivos y arquitectónicos.
En base a nuestra experiencia de vida en la playa creamos para nuestros clientes experiencias de vida enfocados en la eficiencia energética, el aprovechamiento de la luz y la perdurabilidad en el tiempo, conceptos claves en el desarrollo de nuestro proyecto. Hoy en día Altamarea se desarrolla en el ámbito habitacional y comercial. Hemos trabajado los últimos años en el desarrollo de proyectos de hotelería y comercio buscando mediante nuestra propuesta dar una imagen arquitectónica a nuestro entorno.

Altamarea Arquitectura

www.alta-marea.cl

Altamarea Team

Casa GC

Casas THAM

Pichilemu, Chile // Photos © Lucía Fernandez

The project, led by architect Pía Camus in collaboration with the Altamarea team, emerges from the geographical condition between the hill and the sea. Its location and program distribution adapt to the ravine, taking advantage of the topography to create two ways of living: one at a height with views of the sea and another at a lower level connected to a north-facing patio protected from the wind. Access to the main floor divides the common area from the private one. The bedrooms face west, while the kitchen and dining room open onto a cantilevered north terrace. The ground floor houses the social area, with a living room and barbecue area facing the pool, while the service area is connected to the kitchen by an external staircase. The combination of noble materials stands out: concrete, wood, and iron. Its exposed steel structure outlines the entire perimeter of the facade horizontally. The eucalyptus ceiling extends across its entire surface, providing continuity and warmth to each space.

Das von der Architektin Pía Camus in Zusammenarbeit mit dem Team von Altamarea geleitete Projekt entstand aus der geografischen Lage zwischen Hügel und Meer. Die Lage und Verteilung passen sich der Schlucht an und nutzen die Topografie, um zwei Arten des Wohnens zu schaffen: eine in der Höhe mit Blick auf das Meer und eine andere auf niedrigerem Niveau, die mit einem windgeschützten Innenhof verbunden ist. Der Zugang zur Hauptetage trennt den gemeinsamen vom privaten Bereich. Die Schlafzimmer sind nach Westen ausgerichtet, während die Küche und das Esszimmer sich zu einer nördlichen Terrasse mit Überhang öffnen. Das Erdgeschoss beherbergt den sozialen Bereich; Wohnzimmer und Überdachung mit Blick auf den Pool, während der Servicebereich über eine Außentreppe mit der Küche verbunden ist. Besonders hervorzuheben ist die Kombination edler Materialien: Beton, Holz und Eisen. Ihr sichtbares Stahlgerüst zeichnet den gesamten Umfang der Fassade horizontal nach. Die Eukalyptusdecke erstreckt sich über die gesamte Fläche und verleiht jedem Raum Kontinuität und Wärme.

Le projet, dirigé par l'architecte Pía Camus en collaboration avec l'équipe d'Altamarea, tire parti de la situation géographique entre la colline et la mer. Son emplacement et sa distribution s'adaptent à la gorge en utilisant la topographie pour créer deux façons de vivre : une en hauteur avec vue sur la mer et une autre au niveau inférieur reliée à une cour protégée du vent au nord. L'accès à l'étage principal divise la zone commune de la zone privée. Les chambres sont orientées à l'ouest, tandis que la cuisine et la salle à manger s'ouvrent sur une terrasse nord en porte-à-faux. Le rez-de-chaussée abrite la zone sociale ; salon et auvent face à la piscine, tandis que la zone de service est reliée à la cuisine par un escalier extérieur. La combinaison de matériaux nobles, tels que le béton, le bois et le fer, est remarquable. Sa structure en acier apparent dessine tout le périmètre de la façade horizontalement. Le ciel en eucalyptus se projette sur toute sa surface, apportant continuité et chaleur à chaque espace.

El proyecto, liderado por la arquitecta Pía Camus en colaboración con el equipo de Altamarea, nace a partir de la condición geográfica entre el cerro y el mar. Su emplazamiento y distribución se adaptan a la quebrada aprovechando la topografía para crear dos formas de habitar: una en altura con vistas al mar y otra a nivel inferior conectada con un patio norte protegido del viento. El acceso a la planta principal divide el área común de la privada. Los dormitorios quedan orientados hacia el poniente, mientras la cocina y comedor se abren hacia una terraza norte en voladizo. La planta baja alberga el área social: living y cobertizo frente a la piscina, mientras que el área de servicio se conecta a la cocina por una escalera exterior. Destaca la combinación de materiales nobles: hormigón, madera y hierro. Su estructura de acero a la vista dibuja todo el perímetro de la fachada horizontalmente. El cielo en eucaliptus se proyecta en toda su superficie, aportando continuidad y calidez a cada espacio.

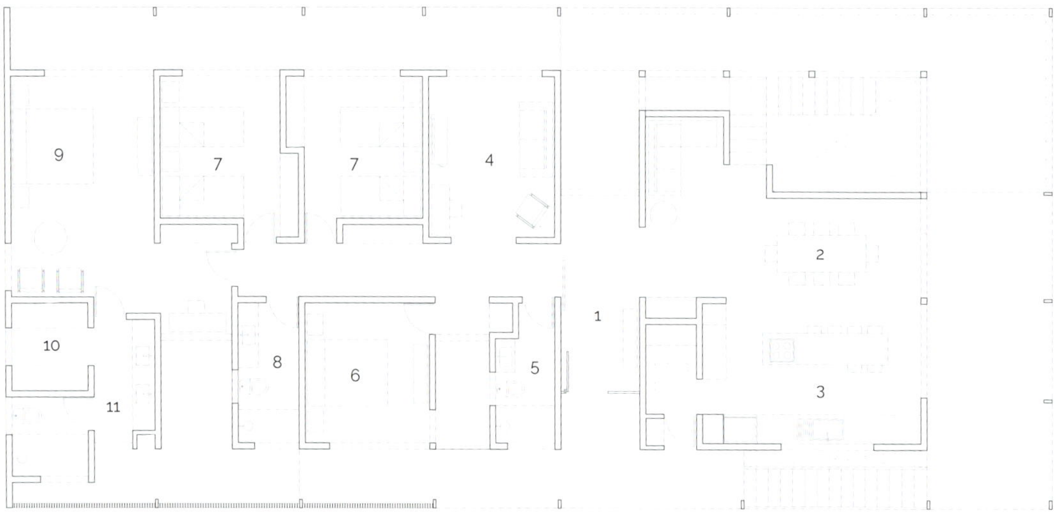

1. Entry
2. Dining
3. Kitchen
4. Family room - study
5. Guest bathroom
6. Guest Room
7. Children's Room
8. Children's Bathroom
9. Main Room
10. Walking closet
11. Main Bath room

Second floor plan

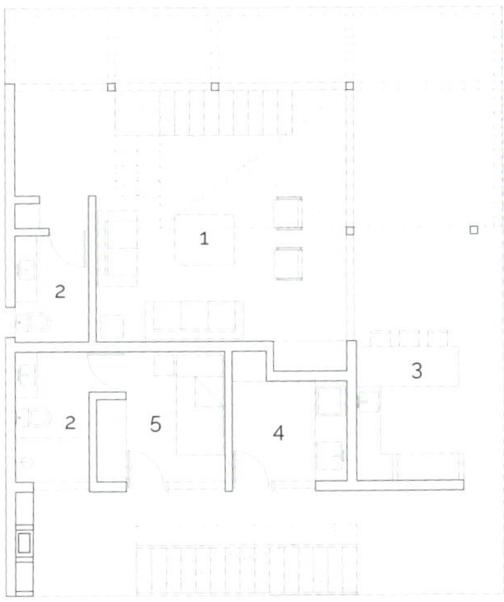

1. Living Room 1
2. Bath room
3. Barbecue area
4. Laundry
5. Room

First floor plan

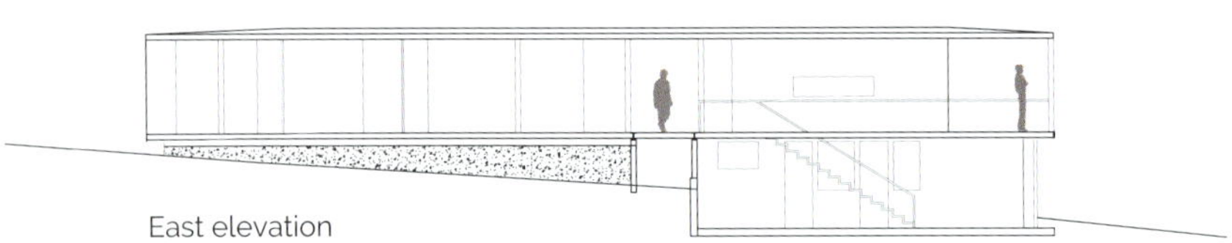

East elevation

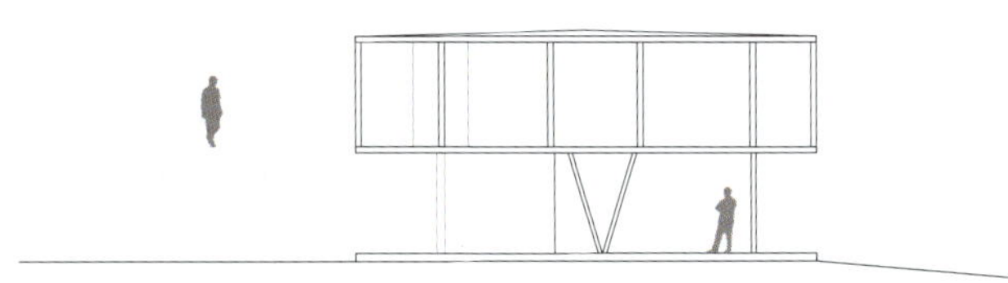

North elevation

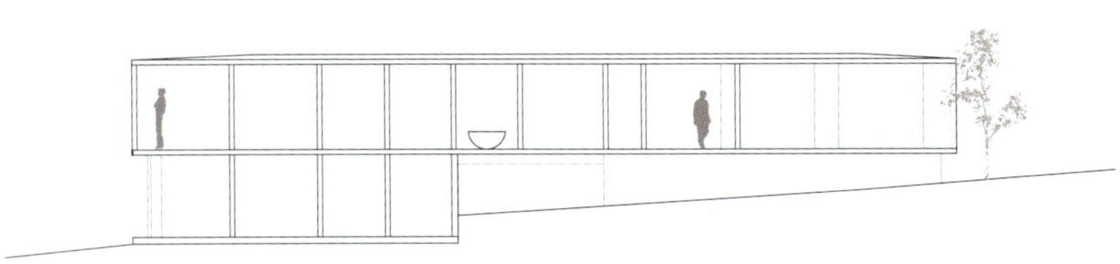

West elevation

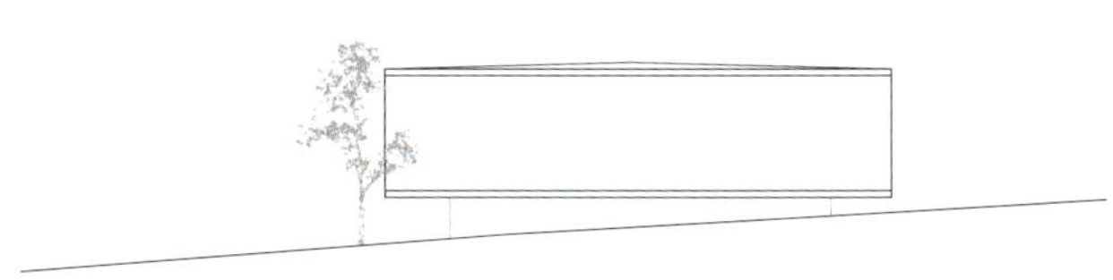

South elevation

Cáhuil, Pichilemu, Chile // Photos © Magdalena León

As a self-commission within our office and in the search for new design challenges, we decided to create a tiny house under the Altamarea concept. The idea is to offer our clients pre-designed projects ready for construction, which are efficient in design, space, and quick to build. The THAM project, "tiny house Altamarea," is our first proposal under these parameters, where in 60 m², we developed the perfect space for a getaway from the city. These houses are developed on 2 floors with double height, integrating common spaces on one level and private space on the second. The materials are characterized by being mostly Radiata pine wood, the prefabricated structure is metal, and the finish is in different tones of the same wood.

Als Eigenauftrag innerhalb unseres Büros und auf der Suche nach neuen Designherausforderungen beschlossen wir, ein Tiny House unter dem Konzept Altamarea zu schaffen. Die Idee ist, unseren Kunden fertige, baubereite Projekte anzubieten, die im Design und Raum effizient sind und schnell gebaut werden können. Das Projekt THAM „Tiny House Altamarea" ist unser erster Vorschlag unter diesen Parametern, bei dem wir auf 60 m² den perfekten Raum für einen Rückzugsort fernab der Stadt entwickelt haben. Diese Häuser erstrecken sich über zwei Etagen mit doppelter Höhe und integrieren gemeinsame Räume auf einer Ebene und privaten Raum im zweiten Stock. Die Materialien zeichnen sich größtenteils durch Kiefernholz aus Radiata aus, die vorgefertigte Struktur besteht aus Metall und die Oberflächen sind in verschiedenen Holztönen gehalten.

En tant que projet interne de notre bureau et à la recherche de nouveaux défis de conception, nous avons décidé de créer une tiny house sous le concept Altamarea. L'idée est d'offrir à nos clients des projets préconçus prêts à construire, efficaces en termes de design et d'espace, et de construction rapide. Le projet THAM « tiny house Altamarea » est notre première proposition selon ces paramètres, où nous avons développé l'espace parfait pour un refuge loin de la ville en 60 m². Ces maisons sont construites sur deux étages avec double hauteur, intégrant des espaces communs à un niveau et un espace privé au second. Les matériaux se caractérisent principalement par du pin Radiata, la structure préfabriquée est en métal et la finition est en différentes teintes du même bois.

Como auto encargo dentro de nuestra oficina y en la búsqueda de nuevos desafíos de diseño decidimos crear una tiny house bajo el concepto Altamarea. La idea es poder ofrecer a nuestros clientes proyectos con diseños pre hechos listos para construir, que sean eficientes en diseño y espacio y de rápida construcción.
El proyecto THAM «tiny house Altamarea» es nuestra primera propuesta bajo estos parámetros, donde en 60 m² desarrollamos el espacio perfecto para un refugio lejos de la ciudad. Estas casas se desarrollan en dos pisos con doble altura, integrando espacios comunes en un nivel y espacio privado en el segundo. Los materiales se caracterizan por ser casi en su totalidad madera de pino Radiata, la estructura prefabricada es de metal y la terminación es en distintos tonos de las misma madera.

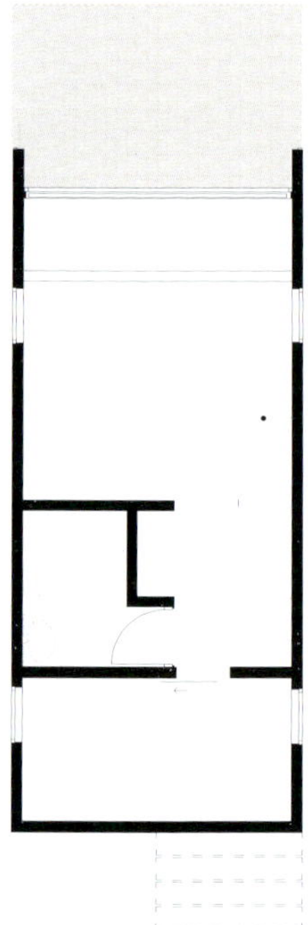

Second floor plan

First floor plan

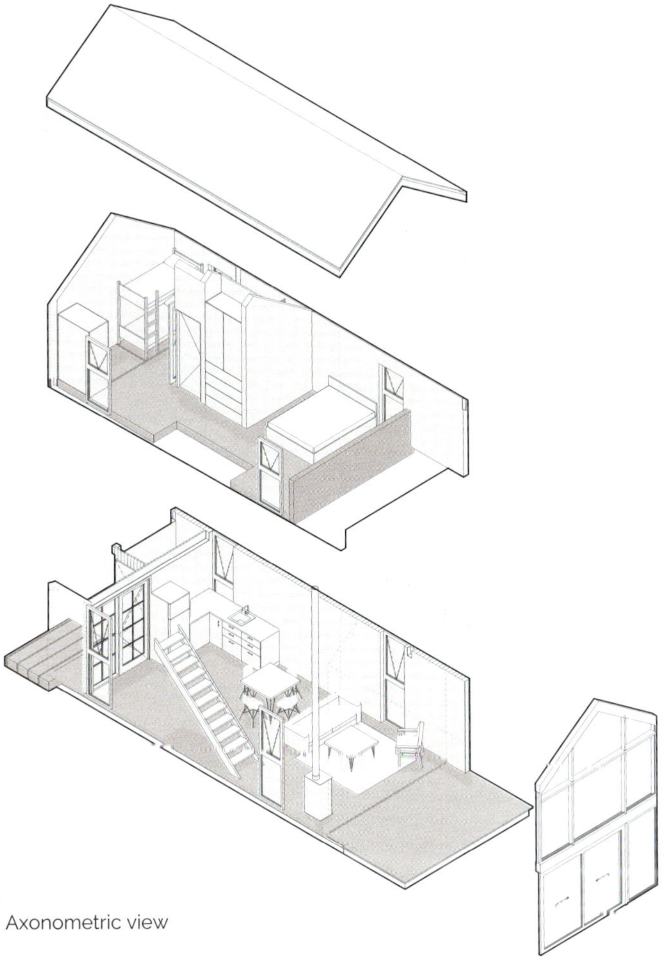

Axonometric view

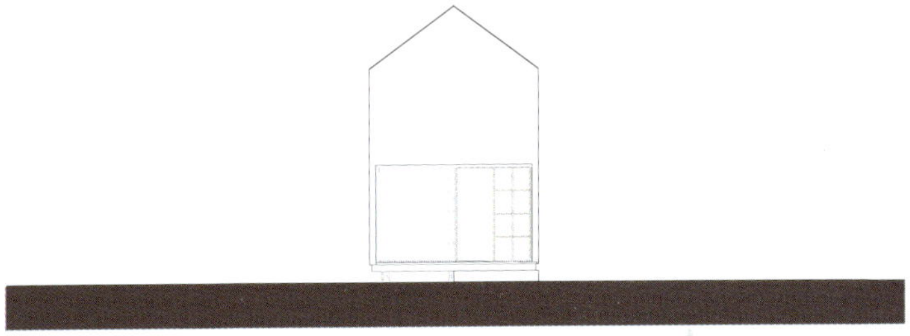

North elevation

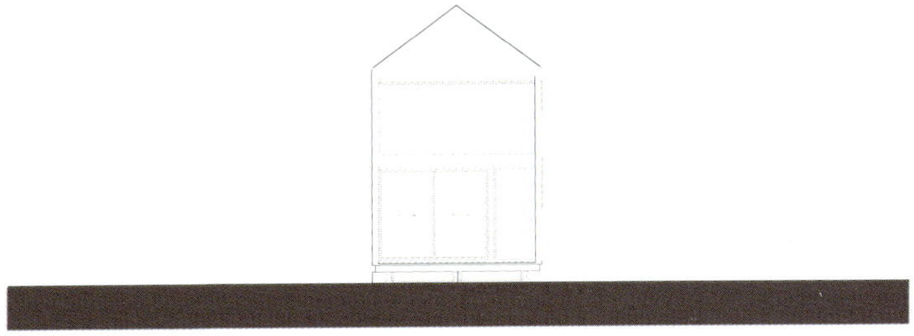

South elevation

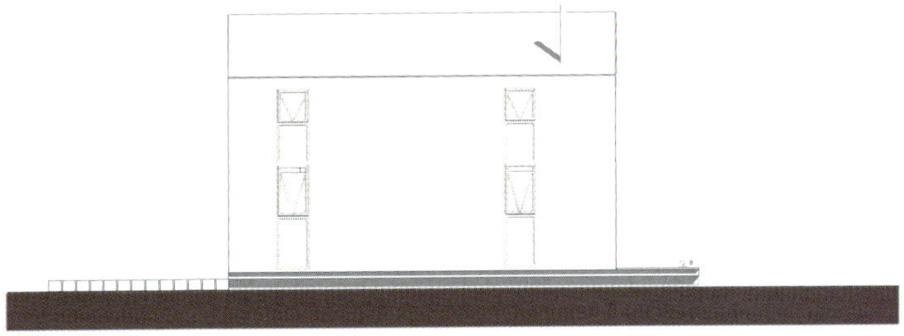

West elevation

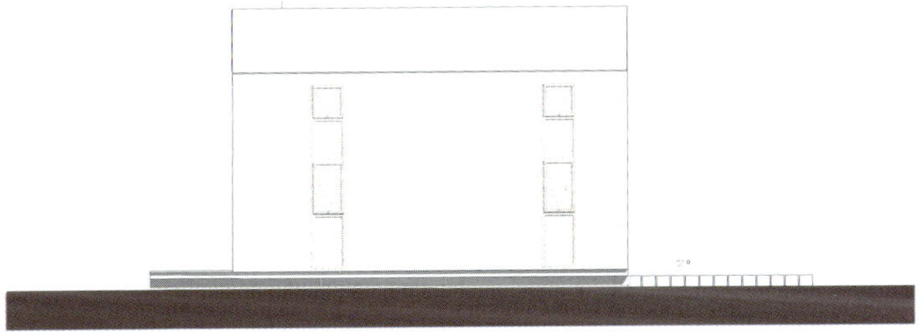

East elevation

Born in Guadalajara, Mexico. Architect by the Instituto Tecnológico y de Estudios Superiores de Occidente, ITESO with an exchange program with the Universidad Iberoamericana de México and with the Master in Architecture degree program from UCLA. Masters Degree of Architecture by the Universidad Politécnica de Cataluña with a scholarship from the same university in the program Master de La Gran Escala, La Arquitectura de los Nuevos Entornos under de direction of Eduard Bru. Finished the Doctorate of Architectural Projects also at the Universidad Politécnica de Cataluña and participated in may projects with Tonet Sunyer in Barcelona. Co founder of Hipogeo in Guadalajara in 2000, he also taught at ITESO University for 2 years in 2002. Founder in 2007 of Alvaro Moragrega / arquitecto he has been selected twice as forerunner for the Obras Cemex award. Honorable mention in the competition "Urban Intervention The Howard S. Wrigh tDesign Ideas Competition for Public Space" in Seattle as well as in the competition of the city's Town Square in Medina del Campo in Spain. He lives and works in Guadalajara, Mexico.

Geboren in Guadalajara, Mexiko. Architekt an der Instituto Tecnológico y de Estudios Superiores de Occidente, ITESO, mit einem Austauschprogramm an der Universidad Iberoamericana de México und einem Master-Abschluss in Architektur an der University of California, Los Angeles (UCLA). Master in Architektur an der Universitat Politècnica de Catalunya mit einem Stipendium derselben Universität im Máster-Programm La Gran Escala, La Arquitectura de los Nuevos Entornos unter der Leitung von Eduard Bru. Abschluss des Doktorats in Architekturprojekten ebenfalls an der Universitat Politècnica de Catalunya und Teilnahme an zahlreichen Projekten mit Tonet Sunyer in Barcelona. Mitbegründer von Hipogeo in Guadalajara im Jahr 2000, unterrichtete auch zwei Jahre lang an der Universidad ITESO im Jahr 2002. Gründer von Alvaro Moragrega/Architekt im Jahr 2007, wurde zweimal als Vorreiter für den Obras Cemex-Preis ausgewählt. Ehrenvolle Erwähnung im Wettbewerb „Urban Intervention The Howard S. Wrigh tDesign Ideas Competition for Public Space" in Seattle sowie im Wettbewerb um den Plaza Mayor der Stadt in Medina del Campo, Spanien. Er lebt und arbeitet in Guadalajara, Mexiko.

Alvaro Moragrega/Architecte, né à Guadalajara, au Mexique. Architecte diplômé de l'Instituto Tecnológico y de Estudios Superiores de Occidente, ITESO, avec un programme d'échange à l'Universidad Iberoamericana de México et titulaire d'une maîtrise en architecture de l'Université de Californie, Los Angeles (UCLA). Maîtrise en architecture de l'Université Politécnique de Catalogne avec une bourse de la même université dans le programme Máster de La Gran Escala, La Arquitectura de los Nuevos Entornos sous la direction d'Eduard Bru. Il a terminé son doctorat en projets architecturaux également à l'Université Politécnique de Catalogne et a participé à de nombreux projets avec Tonet Sunyer à Barcelone. Co-fondateur de Hipogeo à Guadalajara en 2000, il a également enseigné à l'Universidad ITESO pendant 2 ans en 2002. Fondateur en 2007 d'Alvaro Moragrega/Architecte, il a été sélectionné deux fois comme précurseur pour le prix Obras Cemex. Mention honorable dans le concours « Urban Intervention The Howard S. Wrigh tDesign Ideas Competition for Public Space » à Seattle, ainsi que dans le concours de la Plaza Mayor de la ville à Medina del Campo, en Espagne. Il vit et travaille à Guadalajara, au Mexique.

Nació en Guadalajara, México. Arquitecto por el Instituto Tecnológico y de Estudios Superiores de Occidente, ITESO con programas de intercambio con la Universidad Iberoamericana de México y con el programa de posgrado de arquitectura de UCLA. Becado por la Universidad Politécnica de Cataluña cursó el Master de La Gran Escala, La Arquitectura de los Nuevos Entornos bajo la dirección de Eduardo Bru. Cursó el programa de Doctorado de Proyectos Arquitectónicos en la Universidad Politécnica de Cataluña y participó en varios proyectos con Tonet Sunyer en Barcelona. Fue Co fundador de Hipogeo en Guadalajara en el 2000 y se incorporó como profesor de la Universidad ITESO durante dos años en el 2002. En el 2007 fundó Alvaro Moragrega / arquitecto. Ha sido Finalista en dos ocasiones del Premio Obras Cemex. En el concurso «Urban Intervention The Howard S. Wright Design Ideas Competition for Public Space» en Seattle obtuvo mención honorifica así como en el concurso de plaza mayor para Medina del Campo en España. Vive y trabaja en Guadalajara, México.

Alvaro Moragrega / arquitecto

www.alvaromoragrega.com

Alvaro Moragrega

Casa R&R

Casa C&J

Tapalpa, México // Photos © Fernanda Leonel, Juan Diego Taylor

Casa R&R has a clear H scheme, the longest volume has the public areas. A 10 feet high retaining wall that shapes it also helps isolate it from the rest of the house. From the garage you walk into a vestibule to the yoga classroom, laundry and a staircase down to the kitchen and dinging room. This is the central space of the house, it's an abstract box with flat roof, a modern esthetic and transparency; it opens up the south to a terrace with a large dining table and a grill in the retaining wall to the east. Down a staircase, in the second large volume, is the living room. A hallway to the bedrooms has high window panes facing east to bring in the morning light through a private garden edged by a water fountain to the north. At the end of the hallway the master bedroom has it's own patio. Stone, wood, steel, glass and black roof tiles are the only materials used.

Casa R&R hat ein klares H-Schema, wobei der längste Band die öffentlichen Bereiche umfasst. Eine 3 Meter hohe Stützwand hilft, es vom Rest des Hauses zu isolieren. Vom Garagenbereich gelangt man in eine Diele, die zum Yogaraum, zur Waschküche und einer Treppe nach unten zur Küche und zum Esszimmer führt. Dies ist der zentrale Raum des Hauses, eine abstrakte Box mit Flachdach, moderner Ästhetik und Transparenz; sie öffnet sich nach Süden zu einer Terrasse mit einem großen Esstisch und einem Grill an der Stützwand nach Osten hin. Eine Treppe hinunter befindet sich im zweiten großen Band das Wohnzimmer. Ein Gang zu den Schlafzimmern hat hohe Fenster nach Osten hin, um das Morgenlicht durch einen privaten Garten mit einem Wasserbrunnen nach Norden hin eintreten zu lassen. Am Ende des Flurs hat das Hauptschlafzimmer eine eigene Terrasse. Stein, Holz, Stahl, Glas und schwarze Dachziegel sind die einzigen verwendeten Materialien.

Casa R&R a un schéma clair en H, avec le volume le plus long comprenant les zones publiques. Un mur de soutènement de 3 mètres de haut aide à l'isoler du reste de la maison. Depuis le garage, on entre dans un hall qui mène au salon de yoga, à la buanderie et à un escalier descendant vers la cuisine et la salle à manger. C'est l'espace central de la maison, une boîte abstraite avec un toit plat, une esthétique moderne et une transparence ; elle s'ouvre vers le sud sur une terrasse avec une grande table à manger et un barbecue sur le mur de soutènement vers l'est. En descendant un escalier, dans le deuxième grand volume, se trouve le salon. Un couloir vers les chambres a des fenêtres hautes orientées vers l'est pour permettre à la lumière du matin d'entrer à travers un jardin privé bordé par une fontaine d'eau vers le nord. À la fin du couloir, la chambre principale a sa propre terrasse. Pierre, bois, acier, verre et tuiles de toit noir sont les seuls matériaux utilisés.

Casa R&R tiene un esquema claro en H, con el volumen más largo incluyendo las areas publicas. Una pared de contención de 3m de alto ayuda a aislarlo del resto de la casa. Desde el garaje se ingresa a un vestíbulo que conduce al salón de yoga, lavandería y una escalera hacia abajo que lleva a la cocina y el comedor. Este es el espacio central de la casa, es una caja abstracta con techo plano, una estética moderna y transparencia; se abre hacia el sur a una terraza con una gran mesa de comedor y una parrilla en la pared de contención hacia el este. Descendiendo por una escalera, en el segundo volumen grande, se encuentra la sala de estar. Un pasillo hacia los dormitorios tiene ventanales altos orientados hacia el este para permitir que entre la luz de la mañana a través de un jardín privado bordeado por una fuente de agua hacia el norte. Al final del pasillo, el dormitorio principal tiene su propio patio. Piedra, madera, acero, vidrio y tejas de techo negro son los únicos materiales utilizados.

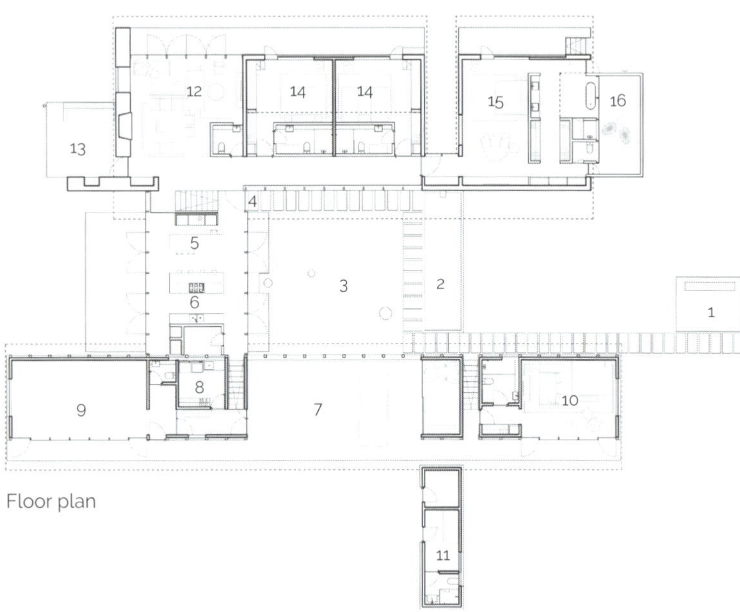

Floor plan

1. Entry
2. Water feature
3. Patio
4. Main entrance
5. Dining
6. Kitchen
7. Parking
8. Laundry
9. Yoga classroom
10. Guest suite
11. Service area
12. Living room
13. Family terrace
14. Children
15. Master bedroom
16. Master bath patio

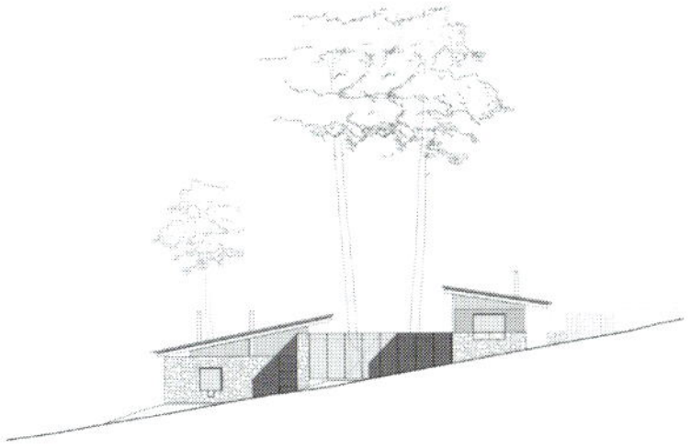

North elevation

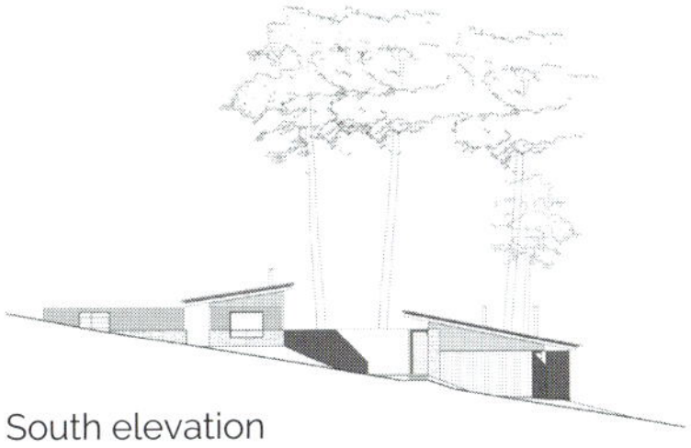

South elevation

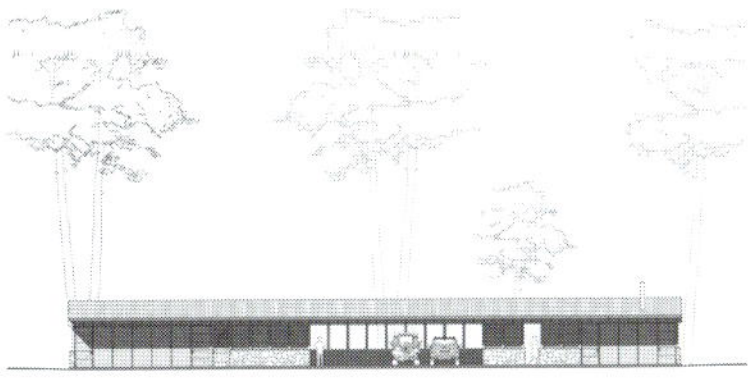

East elevation

West elevation

The house is composed of three separate cabins and a central outdoor space that functions as a foyer. Thus the program is divided in 3: social, master suit and bedrooms. The social cabin has a great room with and mezzanine, garage and service bedroom. The master suite has a small living area and a spa. The bedrooms have a family room, 2 guest rooms, 2 bedrooms with open attic space for the children's guest. All the cabins follow the same building method: elongated brick envelopes with wooden boxes on the inside that protruded to the outside on the short side of the brick boxes with shou sugi ban wood. In the interior all the brick walls are plastered, while all inside divisions are in natural pine wood. The final composition is a clear system used throughout the 3 cabins: brick envelopes with black wood boxes protruding from the short side of the cabins.

Das Haus besteht aus drei separaten Hütten und einem zentralen Außenbereich, der als Eingangshalle fungiert. So ist das Programm in 3 Teile unterteilt: sozial, Hauptsuite und Schlafzimmer. Die Hütte - Wohnzimmer hat einen großen Raum mit einer Galerie, Garage und einem Dienstzimmer. Die Hauptsuite verfügt über ein kleines Wohnzimmer und einen Spa-Bereich. Die Schlafzimmer verfügen über ein Familienzimmer, 2 Gästezimmer, 2 Schlafzimmer mit offenem Dachboden für die Kinder der Gäste. Alle Hütten folgen demselben Konstruktionsprinzip: Langgestreckte Ziegelhüllen mit Holzkisten im Inneren, die auf der kurzen Seite der Kisten mit Shou-Sugi-Ban-Holz hervorstehen. Im Inneren sind alle Ziegelwände verputzt, während die Innenwände aus naturbelassenem Kiefernholz bestehen. Die endgültige Komposition ist ein klares System, das in den 3 Hütten verwendet wird: Ziegelhüllen mit schwarzen Holzkisten, die an der kurzen Seite der Hütten herausragen.

Casa C&J est composée de trois cabanes séparées et d'un espace central en plein air fonctionnant comme un vestibule. Ainsi, le programme est divisé en 3 parties : sociale, suite principale et chambres. La cabane - salle de séjour a un grand espace avec une mezzanine, un garage et une chambre de service. La suite principale a un petit salon et un spa. Les chambres ont une salle familiale, 2 chambres d'hôtes, 2 chambres avec un espace grenier ouvert pour les invités des enfants. Toutes les cabanes suivent le même mode de construction : des enveloppes de briques allongées avec des boîtes en bois à l'intérieur qui débordent vers l'extérieur sur le côté court des boîtes avec du bois shou sugi ban. À l'intérieur, tous les murs de briques sont enduits, tandis que les cloisons internes sont en bois de pin naturel. La composition finale est un système clair utilisé dans les 3 cabanes : des enveloppes de briques avec des boîtes en bois noir dépassant du côté court des cabanes.

La casa está compuesta por tres cabañas separadas y un espacio central al aire libre que funciona como un vestíbulo. Así, el programa se divide en 3: social, suite principal y dormitorios. La cabaña - sala de estar tiene un gran espacio con un entrepiso, garaje y dormitorio de servicio. La suite principal tiene una pequeña sala de estar y un spa. Los dormitorios tienen una sala familiar, 2 habitaciones de huéspedes, 2 dormitorios con espacio de ático abierto para los huéspedes de los niños. Todas las cabañas siguen el mismo método de construcción: sobres de ladrillo alargados con cajas de madera en el interior que sobresalen hacia el exterior en el lado corto de las cajas con madera *shou sugi ban*. En el interior, todas las paredes de ladrillo están enlucidas, mientras que las divisiones internas están en madera de pino natural. La composición final es un sistema claro utilizado en las 3 cabañas: sobres de ladrillo con cajas de madera negra sobresaliendo del lado corto de las cabañas.

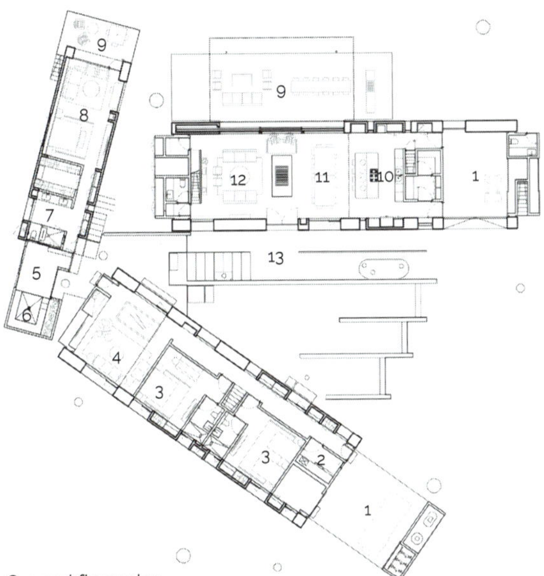

Ground floor plan

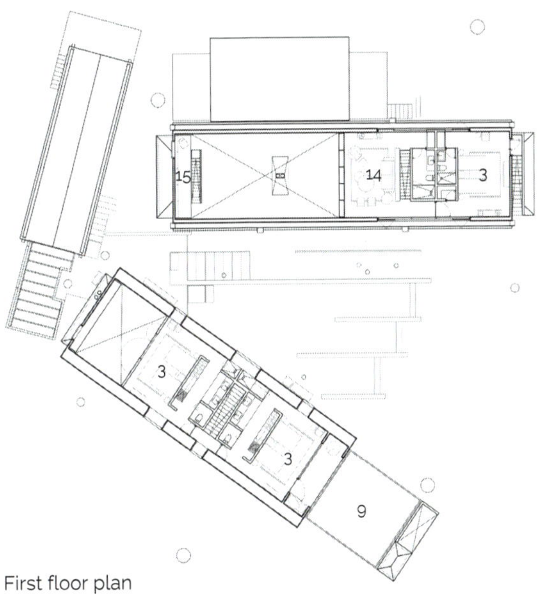

First floor plan

1. Parking
2. Laundry
3. Bedroom
4. Playroom
5. Master bath patio
6. Onsen
7. Master bathroom
8. Master bedroom
9.. Terrace
10. Kitchen
11. Dining
12. Living room
13. Patio
14. Family room
15. Library

We believe that good architecture and urban planning stimulate people. Bring tranquillity or energy. Underline their personality. The spatial experience is in part shaped by associations. Just as a particular smell awakens a personal association in one person, associations form and reinforce the experience of a building.
Architecture and urban planning need to find the right relationship to their surroundings. they need to adapt. give an impulse. trigger an adjustment. We create our projects with a social conscience and we want to bring an added value to people and space. keeping the future in mind is essential for this. buildings must outlive their users. this approach ensures that our projects are grounded both sociologically and ecologically. Without weakening the spatial experience, character or aesthetics. the sustainability of a building or spatial structure depends just as much on how much we love the experience of it.

Wir glauben, dass gute Architektur und Städtebau die Menschen stimulieren. Sie bringen Ruhe oder Energie. Sie unterstreichen ihre Persönlichkeit. Das Raumerlebnis wird teilweise durch Assoziationen bestimmt. So wie ein bestimmter Geruch bei einem Menschen eine persönliche Assoziation auslöst, so prägen und verstärken Assoziationen die Erfahrung eines Gebäudes.
Architektur und Stadtplanung müssen das richtige Verhältnis zu ihrer Umgebung finden, sie müssen sich anpassen, einen Impuls geben, eine Anpassung provozieren. Wir gestalten unsere Projekte mit einem sozialen Gewissen und wollen einen Mehrwert für Menschen und Raum schaffen. Dazu ist es unerlässlich, die Zukunft mit einzubeziehen. Gebäude müssen ihre Nutzer überdauern; dieser Ansatz gewährleistet, dass unsere Projekte sowohl soziologisch als auch ökologisch fundiert sind. Ohne das Raumerlebnis, den Charakter oder die Ästhetik zu schmälern, hängt die Nachhaltigkeit eines Gebäudes oder einer räumlichen Struktur davon ab, wie sehr wir sie erleben..

Nous pensons qu'une bonne architecture et un bon urbanisme stimulent les gens. Ils apportent la tranquillité ou l'énergie. Ils soulignent leur personnalité. L'expérience spatiale est en partie déterminée par des associations. Tout comme une odeur particulière déclenche une association personnelle chez une personne, les associations façonnent et renforcent l'expérience d'un bâtiment.
L'architecture et l'urbanisme doivent trouver la bonne relation avec leur environnement, ils doivent s'adapter, donner une impulsion, provoquer une adaptation. Nous créons nos projets avec une conscience sociale et nous voulons apporter une valeur ajoutée aux personnes et à l'espace. Pour ce faire, il est essentiel de tenir compte de l'avenir. Les bâtiments doivent survivre à leurs utilisateurs ; cette approche garantit que nos projets sont fondés à la fois sur le plan sociologique et sur le plan écologique. Sans affaiblir l'expérience spatiale, le caractère ou l'esthétique, la durabilité d'un bâtiment ou d'une structure spatiale dépend de la mesure dans laquelle nous en apprécions l'expérience.

Creemos que la buena arquitectura y el urbanismo estimulan a las personas. Aportan tranquilidad o energía. Subrayan su personalidad. La experiencia espacial está en parte determinada por las asociaciones. Al igual que un olor determinado despierta una asociación personal en una persona, las asociaciones forman y refuerzan la experiencia de un edificio.
La arquitectura y el urbanismo tienen que encontrar la relación adecuada con su entorno, deben adaptarse, dar un impulso, provocar una adaptación. Creamos nuestros proyectos con conciencia social y queremos aportar un valor añadido a las personas y al espacio. Para ello es esencial tener en cuenta el futuro. Los edificios deben sobrevivir a sus usuarios; este enfoque garantiza que nuestros proyectos tengan un fundamento tanto sociológico como ecológico. Sin debilitar la experiencia espacial, el carácter o la estética, la sostenibilidad de un edificio o de una estructura espacial depende de lo que nos guste la experiencia de la misma.

Atelier Tom Vanhee

www.ateliertomvanhee.be

Tom Vanhee

House with Writing Shed

Old Farm

Wetteren, Belgium // Photos © Ellen Goegebuer

Inspired by the staggered layout of the other constructions in the street, the functions of this house were arranged according to a herringbone design. The three volumes – with the second pushed back in relation to the first, and the third in relation to the second – were finished on the outside with wooden boards whose pattern continues over the adjoining blind walls. The living area spans the different volumes and gains in spatiality thanks to the parents' raised bedroom. The writing shed in the garden provides the creative owner with a space of their own.

Inspirierte von der gestuften Anordnung der anderen Gebäude in der Straße wurden die Funktionen dieses Hauses nach einem Dornendesign organisiert. Die drei Volumina, wobei das zweite im Verhältnis zum ersten zurückgesetzt ist und das dritte im Verhältnis zum zweiten, wurden außen mit Holzbrettern verkleidet, deren Muster über die angrenzenden Blindmauern fortgesetzt wird. Der Wohnbereich erstreckt sich über die verschiedenen Volumina und gewinnt an Geräumigkeit dank des erhöhten Elternschlafzimmers. Das Schreibstudio im Garten bietet dem kreativen Besitzer einen eigenen Raum.

Inspirée par la disposition étagée des autres constructions de la rue, la Casa con Estudio de Escritor a organisé ses fonctions selon un schéma en épi. Les trois volumes, le deuxième en retrait par rapport au premier et le troisième par rapport au deuxième, ont été revêtus à l'extérieur de planches de bois dont le motif se poursuit sur les murs aveugles adjacents. La zone de séjour englobe les différents volumes et gagne en spatialité grâce à la chambre principale surélevée. Le studio d'écriture dans le jardin offre au propriétaire créatif un espace dédié.

Inspirada en la disposición escalonada de las otras construcciones en la calle, las funciones de esta casa fueron organizadas según un diseño de espiga. Los tres volúmenes, con el segundo retrocedido en relación al primero, y el tercero en relación al segundo, fueron terminados en el exterior con tablas de madera cuyo patrón continúa sobre los muros ciegos adyacentes. El área de estar abarca los diferentes volúmenes y gana en espacialidad gracias al dormitorio elevado de los padres. El estudio de escritura en el jardín proporciona al creativo propietario un espacio propio.

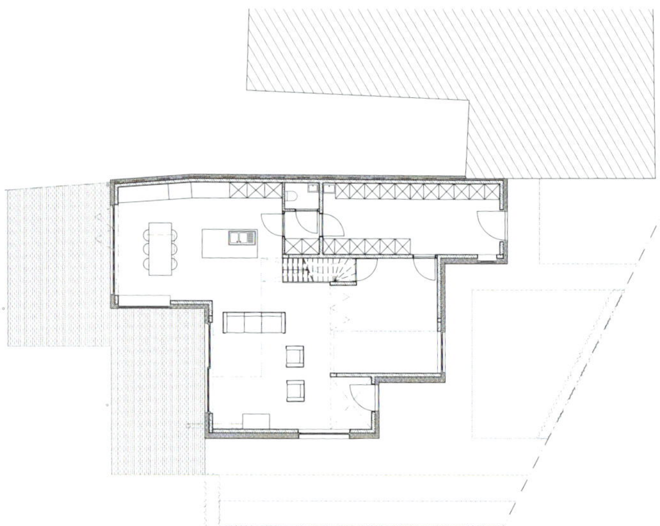

Groud floor plan

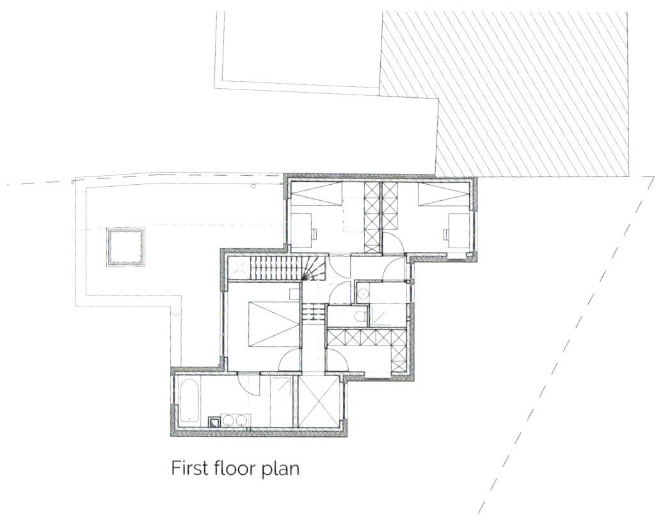

First floor plan

The abstract reconstruction of a dilapidated barn provides the required inward expansion of the main house. The new living spaces in red wood flow into the barn and open up the main house onto the garden. As in the past, arches add rhythm to the abstract volume, and a covered terrace connects the interior courtyard with the rear garden. The stable was renovated with visible concrete additions and serves as a storage area, but an inward expansion of the farm will also be possible in the future with a guest room.

Die abstrakte Rekonstruktion einer verfallenen Scheune stellt eine notwendige interne Erweiterung des Hauptgebäudes dar. Die neuen bewohnbaren Räume aus rotem Holz fließen in die Scheune und öffnen das Hauptgebäude zum Garten hin. Wie in der Vergangenheit verleihen Bögen dem abstrakten Volumen einen Rhythmus, und eine überdachte Terrasse verbindet den Innenhof mit dem hinteren Garten. Der Stall wurde mit sichtbaren Betonergänzungen renoviert und dient als Lagerbereich, aber auch eine interne Erweiterung mit einem Gästezimmer wird in Zukunft möglich sein.

La reconstruction abstraite d'une ancienne grange offre une extension interne nécessaire à la maison principale. Les nouveaux espaces habitables en bois rouge s'écoulent vers la grange et ouvrent la maison principale sur le jardin. Comme dans le passé, les arcs ajoutent du rythme au volume abstrait, et une terrasse couverte relie la cour intérieure au jardin arrière. La grange a été rénovée avec des ajouts de béton apparent et sert de zone de stockage, mais une expansion interne future avec une chambre d'amis est également envisageable.

La reconstrucción abstracta de un granero deteriorado proporciona una extensión interna necesaria de la casa principal. Los nuevos espacios habitables en madera roja fluyen hacia el granero y abren la casa principal al jardín. Como en el pasado, los arcos añaden ritmo al volumen abstracto, y una terraza cubierta conecta el patio interior con el jardín trasero. La cuadra fue renovada con adiciones de hormigón visibles y sirve como área de almacenamiento, pero también será posible una expansión interna en el futuro con una habitación para invitados.

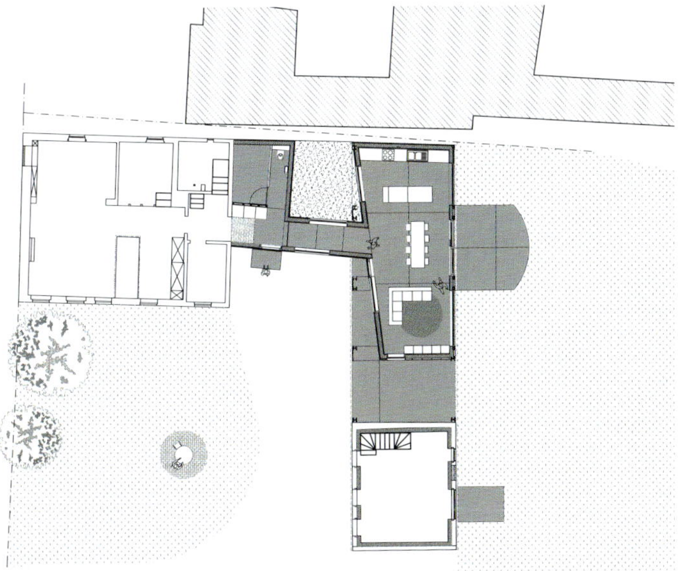

Floor plan

Norwegian born, Erling Berg is an architect and designer with a passion for crafting unique spaces addressing the important relationship between scale, form, light and the use of genuine materials, carefully considering context and functionality. With a rigorous and concept-driven approach, Berg focuses on timeless aesthetics, delicate details and simplicity within the built environment. Berg, who spent the majority of his twenties and his early thirties in California finds inspiration in the horizontal language of mid-century architecture from the region, as well as the Norwegian vernacular and its long building traditions, focusing on wood as the main structural, exterior and interior component. From his studio in Fredrikstad, Norway – Berg continues to to create one of a kind dwellings that often are set in rural surroundings, on sloped and challenging terrain and in touch with nature.

Geboren in Norwegen, ist Erling Berg ein Architekt und Designer mit einer Leidenschaft für die Schaffung einzigartiger Räume, die die wichtige Beziehung zwischen Maßstab, Form, Licht und der Verwendung von authentischen Materialien ansprechen, wobei der Kontext und die Funktionalität sorgfältig berücksichtigt werden. Mit einem rigorosen und konzeptbasierten Ansatz konzentriert sich Berg auf zeitlose Ästhetik, feine Details und Einfachheit in der gebauten Umgebung. Berg, der den Großteil seiner Zwanziger und frühen Dreißigerjahre in Kalifornien verbracht hat, findet Inspiration in der horizontalen Sprache der Architektur der Mitte des 20. Jahrhunderts in der Region sowie im norwegischen Volksmund und seinen langen Bautraditionen, wobei Holz als Hauptstrukturkomponente sowohl im Außen- als auch im Innenbereich im Mittelpunkt steht. Von seinem Studio in Fredrikstad, Norwegen, aus setzt Berg seine Arbeit fort und entwirft oft einzigartige Wohnhäuser, die sich häufig in ländlichen Umgebungen auf schwierigen, geneigten Grundstücken befinden und immer im Kontakt mit der Natur stehen.

Né en Norvège, Erling Berg est un architecte et designer passionné par la création d'espaces uniques qui explorent la relation importante entre l'échelle, la forme, la lumière et l'utilisation de matériaux authentiques, en tenant compte attentivement du contexte et de la fonctionnalité. Avec une approche rigoureuse et conceptuelle, Berg se concentre sur des esthétiques intemporelles, des détails délicats et la simplicité dans l'environnement bâti. Ayant passé la majeure partie de ses vingtaine et du début de ses trente ans en Californie, Berg trouve son inspiration dans le langage horizontal de l'architecture du milieu du XXe siècle de la région, ainsi que dans le vernaculaire norvégien et ses longues traditions de construction, mettant l'accent sur le bois comme composant structurel principal, tant à l'extérieur qu'à l'intérieur. Depuis son studio à Fredrikstad, en Norvège, Berg continue de créer des logements uniques qui sont souvent situés dans des environnements ruraux, sur des terrains pentus et difficiles, toujours en contact avec la nature.

Nacido en Noruega, Erling Berg es un arquitecto y diseñador con una pasión por crear espacios únicos que aborden la importante relación entre la escala, la forma, la luz y el uso de materiales genuinos, considerando cuidadosamente el contexto y la funcionalidad. Con un enfoque riguroso y basado en conceptos, Berg se centra en estéticas atemporales, detalles delicados y simplicidad dentro del entorno construido. Berg, quien pasó la mayor parte de sus veinte años y principios de sus treinta en California, encuentra inspiración en el lenguaje horizontal de la arquitectura de mediados del siglo XX de la región, así como en el vernáculo noruego y sus largas tradiciones de construcción, centrándose en la madera como componente estructural principal, tanto exterior como interior. Desde su estudio en Fredrikstad, Noruega, Berg continúa creando viviendas únicas que a menudo se ubican en entornos rurales, en terrenos inclinados y desafiantes, siempre en contacto con la naturaleza.

Erling Berg

www.erlingberg.com

Erling Berg

I/O Cabin

3 separate volumes are connected by a wooden deck floating above the sloped terrain of solid rock. Under a shared, cantilevered roof, the atrium shaped floor plan creates an "inside/ outside" effect for its purpose as a summer house - using the outdoor spaces as much as the indoors. The summer cabin is wrapped in locally sourced spruce siding, impregnated with an organic wood protection with gray color pigments. The interior walls are all out of white painted, horizontal wood siding that meets a warmer toned floor and ceiling of white oiled spruce - typical to traditional and older cabins on the coast of Norway. The wooden pillars lifting the cabin off the ground are connected with cross-laminated timber beams in the deck, continuing all the way up to the roof construction which copies the structural beams in the deck. A V-shaped wood column caries the weight of the cantilevered roof as a large glass corner opens the main living space to its surrounding natural elements.

Drei separate Volumina sind durch eine Plattform aus Holz verbunden, die über dem geneigten Gelände aus festem Fels schwebt. Unter einem gemeinsamen überhängenden Dach erzeugt der atriumförmige Grundriss einen „drinnen/draußen"-Effekt für die Nutzung als Sommerhaus, wobei die äußeren Räume ebenso wie die inneren genutzt werden. Die Sommerhütte ist in einheimische Fichte gehüllt, die mit einem organischen Holzschutzmittel mit grauen Farbpigmenten imprägniert ist. Die Innenwände sind alle aus weiß gestrichener Holzverkleidung gefertigt, die auf einen wärmeren Ton von geölter weißer Fichte trifft, typisch für traditionelle und alte Hütten an der norwegischen Küste. Die Holzpfosten, die die Hütte vom Boden abheben, sind mit Brettschichtholzbalken auf der Plattform verbunden, die sich bis zur Dachstruktur fortsetzen, die die strukturellen Balken auf der Plattform kopiert. Eine V-förmige Holzsäule trägt das Gewicht des überhängenden Daches, während ein großes Fenster den Hauptwohnbereich zu seinen umgebenden natürlichen Elementen öffnet.

Trois volumes séparés sont reliés par une plateforme en bois flottant sur le terrain incliné de roche solide. Sous un toit en porte-à-faux partagé, le plan d'étage en forme d'atrium crée un effet « intérieur/extérieur » pour une utilisation en tant que maison d'été, utilisant les espaces extérieurs autant que les intérieurs. La cabane d'été est enveloppée de sapin d'origine locale, imprégné d'une protection organique pour le bois avec des pigments de couleur grise. Les murs intérieurs sont tous en lambris de bois peint en blanc, qui rencontre un sol et un plafond de teinte plus chaude en sapin blanc huilé, typique des cabanes traditionnelles et anciennes de la côte norvégienne. Les piliers en bois surélevant la cabine du sol sont reliés par des poutres en bois lamellé-collé sur la plateforme, se poursuivant jusqu'à la structure du toit qui reproduit les poutres structurales sur la plateforme. Une colonne de bois en forme de V supporte le poids du toit en porte-à-faux tandis qu'une grande baie vitrée ouvre l'espace de vie principal à ses éléments naturels environnants.

Tres volúmenes separados quedan conectados por una plataforma de madera que flota sobre el terreno inclinado de roca sólida. Bajo un techo compartido en voladizo, el plano de planta en forma de atrio crea un efecto «dentro/fuera» para su uso como casa de verano. La cabaña de verano está envuelta de abeto de origen local, impregnado con una protección orgánica para madera con pigmentos de color gris. Las paredes interiores están todas hechas de revestimiento de madera pintada de blanco, que se encuentra con un suelo y techo de tono más cálido de abeto blanco aceitado, típico de cabañas tradicionales de la costa Noruega. Los pilares de madera que elevan la cabaña del suelo están conectados con vigas de madera contralaminada en la plataforma, continuando hasta la estructura del techo que copia las vigas estructurales en la plataforma. Una columna de madera en forma de V soporta el peso del techo en voladizo mientras que un gran ventanal abre el espacio de estar principal a sus elementos naturales circundantes.

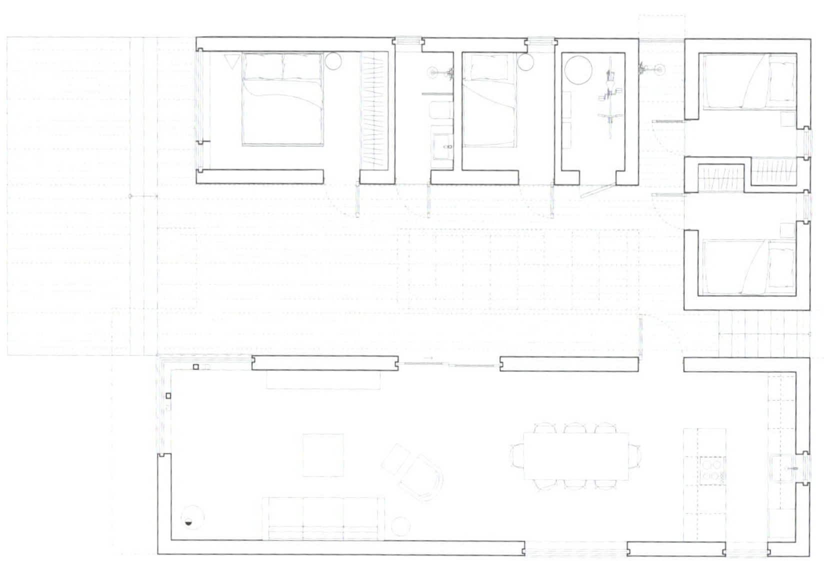

Floor plan

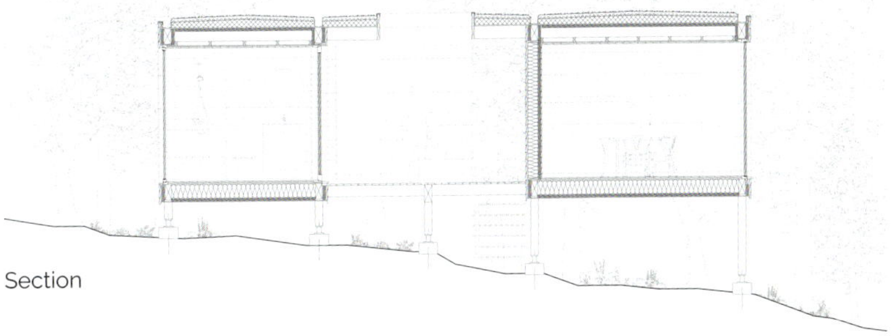

Section

FAMM Architecture, based in Costa Rica, specializes in residential, commercial, and hospitality projects in tropical environments, standing out for its excellence in design, sustainability, and work ethics. From initial sketches to final inspection, the FAMM team actively engages in all stages of the project, ensuring smooth execution and client satisfaction. Their focus on high-quality design is combined with sustainable practices, including passive techniques for energy efficiency and the use of local materials. Transparency and honesty are fundamental in their relationship with clients, working closely to tailor every aspect of the project to their needs and desires, aiming to exceed their expectations in terms of time, cost, and quality.

FAMM Architecture mit Sitz in Costa Rica ist auf Wohn-, Gewerbe- und Gastgewerbeprojekte in tropischen Umgebungen spezialisiert und zeichnet sich durch Exzellenz im Design, Nachhaltigkeit und ethisches Arbeiten aus. Vom ersten Entwurf bis zur endgültigen Inspektion ist das FAMM-Team in allen Projektphasen aktiv involviert und gewährleistet einen reibungslosen Ablauf und die Zufriedenheit der Kunden. Ihr Schwerpunkt auf hochwertigem Design wird mit nachhaltigen Praktiken kombiniert, einschließlich passiver Techniken zur Energieeffizienz und Verwendung lokaler Materialien. Transparenz und Ehrlichkeit sind grundlegend für ihre Beziehung zu den Kunden, indem sie eng zusammenarbeiten, um jeden Aspekt des Projekts an deren Bedürfnisse und Wünsche anzupassen und deren Erwartungen in Bezug auf Zeit, Kosten und Qualität zu übertreffen.

FAMM Architecture, basée au Costa Rica, est spécialisée dans les projets résidentiels, commerciaux et hôteliers dans les environnements tropicaux, se distinguant par son excellence en design, durabilité et éthique de travail. Des croquis initiaux à l'inspection finale, l'équipe de FAMM est activement impliquée à toutes les étapes du projet, garantissant une exécution fluide et la satisfaction du client. Leur approche de haute qualité en matière de conception est associée à des pratiques durables, y compris des techniques passives pour l'efficacité énergétique et l'utilisation de matériaux locaux. La transparence et l'honnêteté sont essentielles dans leur relation avec les clients, et ils s'efforcent d'établir des partenariats à long terme basés sur la confiance et le respect mutuel.

FAMM Architecture, con sede en Costa Rica, se especializa en proyectos residenciales, comerciales y de hospitalidad en entornos tropicales, destacándose por su excelencia en diseño, sostenibilidad y ética laboral. Desde los bocetos iniciales hasta la inspección final, el equipo de FAMM se involucra activamente en todas las etapas del proyecto, garantizando una ejecución fluida y la satisfacción del cliente. Su enfoque en diseño de alta calidad se combina con prácticas sostenibles, incluyendo técnicas pasivas para la eficiencia energética y el uso de materiales locales. La transparencia y la honestidad son fundamentales en su relación con los clientes, trabajando en estrecha colaboración para adaptar cada aspecto del proyecto a sus necesidades y deseos, con el objetivo de superar sus expectativas en tiempo, costo y calidad.

FAMM Arquitectura

www.fammarq.com

Felipe Apestegui
Mariano Mesalles

Casa Jungla

The design and conceptualization of Jungle House involve a continuous dialogue between the natural environment and the dwelling. Residents experience a transition between indoor and outdoor spaces by crossing thresholds that expose or shelter them in relation to nature. The house is distributed around a perimeter wall of local fieldstone, providing privacy while keeping the rear facade open to the landscape. The social program is concentrated on the ground floor, with a kitchen, living room, and dining room in a single space that opens up to views of the trees, the pool, and the terrace. The secondary bedrooms share a bathroom and are oriented towards outdoor spaces. On the lower level, a living area with access to the garden, laundry room, and equipment room is created. An additional level with concrete beams and an external staircase was incorporated, where the master bedroom with a bathroom, balcony, and planter is located. Openings at both ends provide natural light, cross ventilation, and views of the jungle.

Das Design und die Konzeptualisierung des Casa Jungla basieren auf einem Dialog zwischen der natürlichen Umgebung und dem Wohnraum. Das Haus ist um eine Perimeterwand aus örtlichem Stein gebaut, die Privatsphäre bietet und die Rückseite des Hauses zum Landschaftspanorama hin offen lässt. Das Programm konzentriert sich im Erdgeschoss mit Küche, Wohnzimmer und Esszimmer in einem offenen Raum, der sich zur Aussicht auf Bäume, Pool und Terrasse hin öffnet. Die sekundären Schlafzimmer teilen sich ein Badezimmer und sind zum Außenbereich ausgerichtet. Auf der unteren Ebene befindet sich ein Wohnbereich mit Zugang zum Garten, zur Wäscherei und zum Maschinenraum. Eine zusätzliche Ebene mit Betonträgern und einer Außentreppe wurde hinzugefügt, auf der sich das Hauptschlafzimmer mit Bad, Balkon und Pflanzgefäß befindet. Öffnungen an beiden Enden bieten natürliches Licht, Querlüftung und Ausblicke auf den Dschungel.

La conception et la conceptualisation de la Maison Jungla découlent d'un dialogue continu entre l'environnement naturel et l'habitat. Les résidents vivent une transition entre les espaces intérieurs et extérieurs en traversant des seuils qui exposent ou protègent la relation avec la nature. La maison est distribuée autour d'un mur périmétral en pierre de mollejón local, assurant l'intimité tout en maintenant la façade arrière ouverte sur le paysage. Le programme se concentre au rez-de-chaussée, avec une cuisine, un salon et une salle à manger dans un espace ouvert offrant une vue sur les arbres, la piscine et la terrasse. Les chambres secondaires partagent une salle de bains et sont orientées vers les espaces extérieurs. Au niveau inférieur, une zone de séjour avec accès au jardin, une buanderie et une salle d'équipements sont créées. Un niveau supplémentaire avec des poutres en béton et un escalier extérieur est ajouté, abritant la chambre principale avec salle de bains, balcon et pot de fleurs. Des ouvertures aux deux extrémités fournissent une lumière naturelle, une ventilation croisée et des vues sur la jungle.

El diseño y conceptualización de Casa Jungla parte un diálogo continuo entre el entorno natural y la vivienda. Los residentes experimentan una transición entre espacios interiores y exteriores al atravesar umbrales que exponen o resguardan la relación con la naturaleza. La casa se distribuye alrededor de un muro perimetral de piedra de mollejón local, proporcionando privacidad y manteniendo la fachada trasera abierta al paisaje. El programa se concentra en la planta baja, con cocina, sala y comedor en un espacio único que se abre hacia la vista de los árboles, la piscina y la terraza. Los dormitorios secundarios comparten un baño y se orientan hacia los espacios exteriores. En el nivel inferior se crea un área de estar con acceso al jardín, lavandería y sala de equipos. Se incorporó un nivel adicional con vigas de hormigón y escalera exterior, donde se encuentra el dormitorio principal con baño, balcón y maceta. Aperturas en ambos extremos proporcionan luz natural, ventilación cruzada y vistas a la jungla.

Section

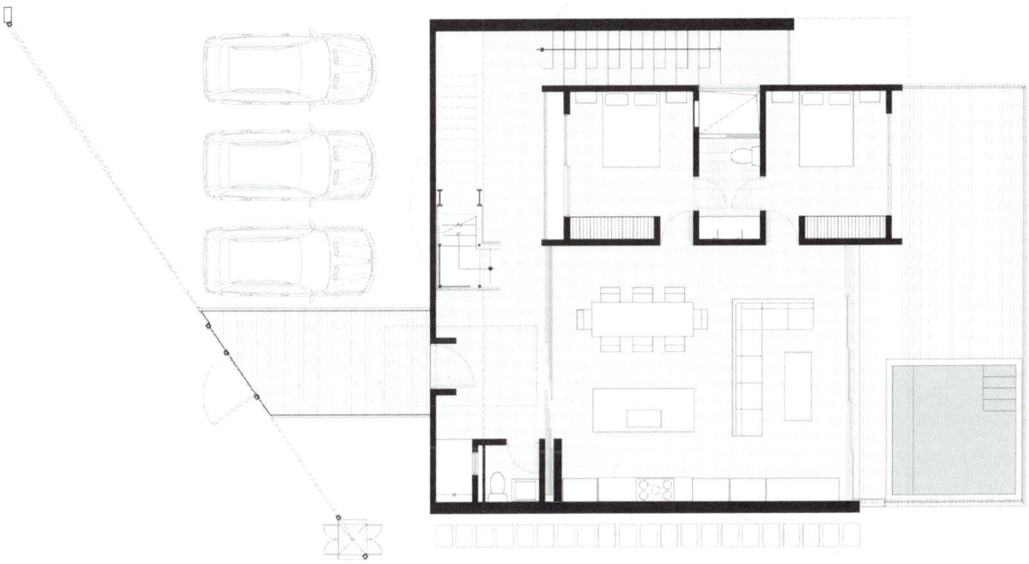

First floor plan

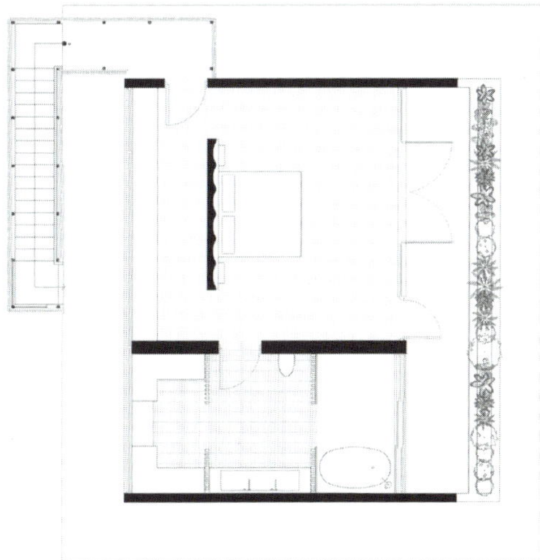

Second floor plan

Nils Finne, AIA, is principal of the award-winning FINNE Architects in Seattle. His residential work has been widely published locally and nationally in over 100 books and magazines. FINNE Architects has been recognized as one of the best Seattle design firms by local and national media. In addition to architecture, Nils has been involved in the design and fabrication of more than 80 pieces of furniture, lighting and hardware. He is known for highly crafted, sustainable, modern residential architecture. Prior to founding FINNE Architects in 1991, Nils was a Senior Associate at Richard Meier and Partners, and served as Project Architect for the $350 million Getty Museum, approximately one-third of the $1 billion Getty Center complex in Los Angeles. Nils received a M.Arch degree in from Harvard Graduate School of Design in 1980. He has been practicing sustainable design for over 25 years, and is a member of the U.S. Green Building Council..

Nils Finne, AIA, ist Direktor der preisgekrönten Finne Architects in Seattle. Seine Arbeiten im Wohnraumbereich wurden lokal und national in über 100 Büchern und Zeitschriften veröffentlicht. Finne Architects wurde von den lokalen und nationalen Medien als eines der besten Planungsunternehmen in Seattle gelobt. Neben der Architektur war Nils auch an der Planung und Herstellung von mehr als 80 Möbeln, Leuchten und Alltagsgegenständen beteiligt. Er ist bekannt für seine hochmoderne, nachhaltige und moderne Wohnarchitektur. Vor der Gründung von Finne Architects im Jahr 1991 war Nils Senior Associate bei Richard Meier and Partners und arbeitete als Projektarchitekt für das 350 Millionen Dollar teure Getty Museum, das etwa ein Drittel des eine Milliarde Dollar teuren „Getty Center"-Komplexes in Los Angeles ausmacht. Nils erhielt 1980 einen M.Arch-Abschluss von der Harvard Graduate School of Design. Er praktiziert seit über 25 Jahren nachhaltiges Design und ist Mitglied des US Green Building Council.

Nils Finne, AIA, est président de FINNE Architects, cabinet primé de Seattle. Son travail résidentiel a fait l'objet de publications dans plus de 100 livres et magasines locaux et nationaux. FINNE Architects est reconnu comme étant l'une des meilleures compagnies de design de Seattle par les médias locaux et nationaux. En plus de l'architecture, Nils a été impliqué dans le design et la fabrication de plus de 80 articles de mobilier, d'éclairage et d'équipement. Il est connu pour une architecture résidentielle moderne, durable, et extrêmement élaborée. Avant de fonder FINNE Architects en 1991, Nils était Associé principal chez Richard Meier & Partners, et a travaillé comme architecte de projet pour le Getty Museum, projet de 350 millions d'USD, approximativement équivalent à un tiers du complexe de 1 milliard du Getty Center à Los Angeles. Il a obtenu son diplôme d'architecture à l'École de design de Harvard en 1980. Il pratique le design durable depuis plus de 25 ans, et fait partie du Green Building Council des États-Unis.

Nils Finne, AIA, es el director del galardonado estudio FINNE Architects en Seattle. Su trabajo residencial ha sido ampliamente publicado a nivel local y nacional en más de 100 libros y revistas. FINNE Architects ha sido reconocida como una de las mejores firmas de diseño de Seattle por los medios de comunicación locales y nacionales. Además de la arquitectura, Nils ha participado en el diseño y fabricación de más de 80 piezas de mobiliario, iluminación y herrajes. Es conocida por su arquitectura residencial altamente artesanal, sostenible y moderna. Antes de fundar FINNE Architects en 1991, Nils fue Socio Senior en Richard Meier and Partners, y fue el Arquitecto de Proyecto para el Museo Getty con un presupuesto de 350 millones de dólares, aproximadamente un tercio del complejo Getty Center en los Ángeles que costó 1 billón de dólares. Nils recibió su título de Máster en Arquitectura en la Harvard Graduate School of Design en 1980. Ha estado trabajando en diseño sostenible durante más de 25 años y es miembro del Consejo de Edificios Ecológicos de los Estados Unidos.

FINNE Architects

www.finne.com

Nils Finne, Principal
Christopher Graesser, Senior associate
Cassandra Isaacson, Associate

Bainbridge House

Bainbridge Island, Washington, USA // Photos © Benjamin Benschneider

The Bainbridge House is a secluded sanctuary on a wooded 3-acre island site. A 500-ft driveway winds through the woods up to the house, located in a clearing at the top of a gentle hill. The house opens to a gently sloping meadow on the south side of the clearing.
The living pavilion ceiling has a dense pattern of exposed wood beams, interrupted by five shafts of light coming from roof light monitors. Each light monitor is rotated slightly from the orthogonal geometry of the wood beams, so there is a sense of movement across the wood ceiling. The light monitors in the ceiling begin at the kitchen and then unfold as the visitor moves through the space. The dining table is placed across from the kitchen, with large sliding glass doors opening to a raised terrace overlooking the meadow.

Das Bainbridge House ist ein abgeschiedener Zufluchtsort auf einem bewaldeten 3-Hektar-Inselgrundstück. Eine 500 Fuß lange Zufahrt schlängelt sich durch den Wald bis zum Haus, das auf einer Lichtung auf der Spitze eines sanften Hügels liegt. Das Haus öffnet sich zu einer sanft abfallenden Wiese an der Südseite der Lichtung.
Die Decke des Wohnpavillons besteht aus einem dichten Muster freiliegender Holzbalken, die von fünf Lichtschächten unterbrochen werden, die von Dachlichtmonitoren stammen. Jeder Lichtmonitor ist gegenüber der orthogonalen Geometrie der Holzbalken leicht gedreht, so dass ein Gefühl der Bewegung über die Holzdecke entsteht. Die Lichtmonitore in der Decke beginnen in der Küche und entfalten sich dann, während der Besucher sich durch den Raum bewegt. Der Esstisch befindet sich gegenüber der Küche, und große Glasschiebetüren führen auf eine erhöhte Terrasse mit Blick auf die Wiese.

La Maison Bainbridge est un sanctuaire isole sur un terrain boisé de 3 acres. Une allée de 500 pieds serpente à travers les bois jusqu'à la maison, située dans une clairière au sommet d'une colline douce.
La maison s'ouvre sur une prairie en pente douce du côté sud de la clairière. Le plafond du pavillon de vie présente un motif dense de poutres en bois exposées, interrompu par cinq puits de lumière provenant de moniteurs de toit. Chaque moniteur de lumière est légèrement incliné par rapport à la géométrie orthogonale des poutres en bois, créant ainsi un sentiment de mouvement à travers le plafond en bois. Les moniteurs de lumière dans le plafond commencent à la cuisine et se déplient à mesure que le visiteur se déplace dans l'espace. La table à manger est placée en face de la cuisine, avec de grandes portes coulissantes en verre s'ouvrant sur une terrasse surélevée donnant sur la prairie.

La Casa Bainbridge es un santuario aislado en una isla arbolada de 1,5 hectáreas. Un camino de 1.500 m serpentea por el bosque hasta la casa, situada en un claro en lo alto de una suave colina. La casa se abre a un prado de suave pendiente en el lado sur del claro.
El techo del pabellón tiene un denso patrón de vigas de madera a la vista, interrumpido por cinco haces de luz procedentes de los monitores de luz del techo los cuales están ligeramente girados con respecto a la geometría ortogonal de las vigas de madera, por lo que hay una sensación de movimiento a través del techo. Empiezan en la cocina y se van desplegando a medida que el visitante se desplaza por el espacio. La mesa del comedor está situada frente a la cocina, con grandes puertas correderas de cristal que dan a una terraza elevada con vistas al prado.

For us, personal happiness means making other people happier and more satisfied within their homes. It is a privilege for us to be able to live our vocation as a profession. With dedication and joy to beauty, we are able to tailor each and every one of our projects to the needs of the residents and implement them with love down to the last detail. The focus of our work is the holistic view of a space, always in connection with the people for whom it is intended. We ensure that sensuality, harmony and haptic experiences create unique moments of well-being. We compose light and space, materials, colours and shapes, details and transitions into an overall picture. This enables sustainable spatial experiences, as the love within the space reflects on its residents. Working with wood as a material is very close to our hearts, as it implies both regionality and nature.

Für uns bedeutet persönliches Glück, andere Menschen glücklicher und zufriedener in ihren Häusern zu machen. Es ist für uns ein Privileg, unsere Berufung als Beruf ausüben zu können. Mit Hingabe und Freude an der Schönheit sind wir in der Lage, jeden unserer Projekte an die Bedürfnisse der Bewohner anzupassen und sie bis ins kleinste Detail mit Liebe umzusetzen. Im Mittelpunkt unserer Arbeit steht die ganzheitliche Vision eines Raumes, immer in Verbindung mit den Menschen, für die er bestimmt ist. Wir stellen sicher, dass Sinnlichkeit, Harmonie und taktile Erfahrungen einzigartige Wohlfühlmomente schaffen. Wir komponieren Licht und Raum, Materialien, Farben und Formen, Details und Übergänge zu einem Gesamtbild. Dies ermöglicht nachhaltige Raumerfahrungen, da die Liebe im Raum sich in seinen Bewohnern widerspiegelt. Die Arbeit mit Holz als Material liegt uns sehr am Herzen, da sie sowohl Regionalität als auch Natur impliziert.

Pour nous, le bonheur personnel signifie rendre les autres plus heureux et plus satisfaits dans leurs foyers. Pour nous, c'est un privilège de pouvoir vivre notre vocation en tant que profession. Avec dévouement et joie pour la beauté, nous sommes capables d'adapter chacun de nos projets aux besoins des résidents et de les réaliser avec amour jusqu'au moindre détail. Le centre de notre travail est la vision globale d'un espace, toujours en connexion avec les personnes auxquelles il est destiné. Nous nous assurons que la sensualité, l'harmonie et les expériences tactiles créent des moments uniques de bien-être. Nous composons la lumière et l'espace, les matériaux, les couleurs et les formes, les détails et les transitions dans une image d'ensemble. Cela permet des expériences spatiales durables, car l'amour à l'intérieur de l'espace se reflète dans ses résidents. Travailler avec le bois comme matériau nous est très proche, car il implique à la fois la régionalité et la nature.

Para nosotros, la felicidad personal significa hacer que otras personas sean más felices y estén más satisfechas en sus hogares. Para nosotros es un privilegio poder vivir nuestra vocación como profesión. Con dedicación y alegria por la belleza, somos capaces de adaptar todos y cada uno de nuestros proyectos a las necesidades de los residentes y llevarlos a cabo con amor hasta el último detalle. El centro de nuestro trabajo es la visión global de un espacio, siempre en conexión con las personas a las que va destinado. Nos aseguramos de que la sensualidad, la armonia y las experiencias táctiles creen momentos únicos de bienestar. Componemos luz y espacio, materiales, colores y formas, detalles y transiciones en una imagen de conjunto. Esto permite experiencias espaciales sostenibles, ya que el amor dentro del espacio se refleja en sus residentes. Trabajar con la madera como material nos resulta muy cercano, ya que implica tanto regionalidad como naturaleza.

GO INTERIORS

www.go-interiors.ch

Nicole Gottschall

Penthouse Davos

"A home connected to a place and filled with the love of family and friends." With this in mind, we were able to design an exclusive vacation apartment, which impresses with its timeless alpine chic. A 6-room apartment has been created on an area of approx. 380 m², in which each room has its own en-suite bathroom. The residents and their guests were to be given the feeling of being in a home away from home. The area for social interaction was skillfully separated from the sleeping areas, creating a sense of increased privacy for vacation guests in particular. The area of the apartment where everyone comes together has been divided up very generously, with the kitchen and the transverse fireplace acting as a room divider and allowing more coziness. With carefully selected materials that create a connection to the beautiful natural surroundings of the Swiss mountains, rooms full of positive energy and relaxed power have been created.

„Ein Zuhause, das mit einem Ort verbunden ist und voller Liebe von Familie und Freunden ist". Mit diesem Gedanken im Hinterkopf konnten wir ein exklusives Ferienapartment entwerfen, das durch seinen zeitlosen alpinen Chic besticht. Es wurde ein Apartment mit 6 Zimmern auf einer Fläche von ca. 380 m² geschaffen, in dem jedes Zimmer über ein eigenes Badezimmer verfügt. Die Bewohner und ihre Gäste sollten das Gefühl haben, sich in einem Zuhause fernab von zu Hause zu befinden. Der soziale Interaktionsbereich wurde geschickt von den Schlafbereichen getrennt, um ein größeres Gefühl von Privatsphäre zu schaffen, insbesondere für Urlaubsgäste. Der Bereich der Wohnung, in dem sich alle versammeln, wurde großzügig unterteilt, wobei die Küche und der quer liegende Kamin als Raumteiler fungieren und eine größere Intimität ermöglichen. Durch sorgfältig ausgewählte Materialien, die eine Verbindung zur wunderschönen natürlichen Umgebung der Schweizer Berge herstellen, wurden Räume voller positiver Energie und entspannender Kraft geschaffen.

« Un foyer connecté à un lieu et rempli de l'amour de la famille et des amis ». Avec cela à l'esprit, nous avons été en mesure de concevoir un appartement exclusif de vacances, qui impressionne par son style alpin intemporel chic. Un appartement de 6 pièces a été créé sur une superficie d'environ 380 m², où chaque chambre a sa propre salle de bain. Les résidents et leurs invités devaient se sentir comme chez eux loin de chez eux. La zone d'interaction sociale a été habilement séparée des zones de couchage, créant une sensation d'intimité accrue, surtout pour les vacanciers. La zone de l'appartement où tout le monde se réunit a été généreusement divisée, avec la cuisine et la cheminée transversale agissant comme séparateurs d'espaces et permettant une plus grande intimité. Avec des matériaux soigneusement sélectionnés qui créent un lien avec le magnifique environnement naturel des montagnes suisses, des chambres pleines d'énergie positive et de pouvoir relaxant ont été créées.

«Un hogar conectado a un lugar y lleno del amor de la familia y los amigos». Con esto en mente, hemos sido capaces de diseñar un exclusivo apartamento de vacaciones, que impresiona por su estilo atemporal chic alpino. Se ha creado un apartamento de 6 habitaciones en una superficie aproximada de 380 m², en el que cada habitación tiene su propio cuarto de baño. Los residentes y sus invitados debían tener la sensación de estar en un hogar lejos de casa. El área de interacción social se separó hábilmente de las zonas de dormitorio, creando una sensación de mayor intimidad, sobre todo para los huéspedes de vacaciones. La zona del apartamento donde se reúne todo el mundo se ha dividido de forma muy generosa, con la cocina y la chimenea transversal actuando como separador de ambientes y permitiendo una mayor intimidad. Con materiales cuidadosamente seleccionados que crean una conexión con el bello entorno natural de las montañas suizas, se han conseguido habitaciones llenas de energía positiva y poder relajante.

Founded in 2010, IDEE Architects was established by architects Tran Ngoc Linh and Nguyen Huy Hai, known for their design projects in resorts and residential homes. Over the years, the office has gained recognition with numerous awards and many projects featured in specialized magazines worldwide.
Our design philosophy, "Simplicity," focuses on purity and simplicity in architecture. IDEE practices architecture on projects ranging from small to large scales. We are committed to sustainability, nature, and considerate of the impact of design on environmental improvement and human awareness. We also prioritize the application of advanced solutions and new materials to explore the future direction of architecture.

Gegründet im Jahr 2010, wurde IDEE Architects von den Architekten Tran Ngoc Linh und Nguyen Huy Hai etabliert, die für ihre Designprojekte in Resorts und Wohnhäusern bekannt sind. Im Laufe der Jahre hat das Büro mit zahlreichen Preisen Anerkennung gefunden und viele Projekte wurden in Fachzeitschriften auf der ganzen Welt vorgestellt.
Unsere Designphilosophie, „Einfachheit", konzentriert sich auf die Reinheit und Einfachheit in der Architektur. IDEE praktiziert Architektur in Projekten von klein bis groß. Wir sind verpflichtet, Nachhaltigkeit, Natur und den Einfluss des Designs auf die Umweltverbesserung und das menschliche Bewusstsein zu berücksichtigen. Wir priorisieren auch die Anwendung fortschrittlicher Lösungen und neuer Materialien, um die zukünftige Richtung der Architektur zu erkunden.

IDEE Architects, fondé en 2010 par les architectes Tran Ngoc Linh et Nguyen Huy Hai, est connu pour ses projets de design dans les stations balnéaires et les maisons résidentielles. Au fil des ans, le cabinet a remporté de nombreux prix et a vu de nombreux projets présentés dans des magazines spécialisés du monde entier.
Notre philosophie de design, « Simplicité », se concentre sur la pureté et la simplicité en architecture. IDEE pratique l'architecture dans des projets allant de petite à grande échelle. Nous sommes engagés envers la durabilité, la nature et nous considérons l'impact de la conception sur l'amélioration de l'environnement et la conscience humaine. Nous donnons également la priorité à l'application de solutions avancées et de nouveaux matériaux pour explorer la direction future de l'architecture.

Fundada en 2010, IDEE Architects fue establecida por los arquitectos Tran Ngoc Linh y Nguyen Huy Hai, conocidos por sus proyectos de diseño en resorts y casas residenciales. A lo largo de los años, la oficina ha ganado reconocimiento con numerosos premios y muchos proyectos presentados en revistas especializadas en todo el mundo.
Nuestra filosofía de diseño, «Simplicidad», se centra en la pureza y simplicidad en la arquitectura. IDEE practica la arquitectura en proyectos que van desde pequeña a gran escala. Estamos comprometidos con la sostenibilidad, la naturaleza y consideramos el impacto del diseño en la mejora ambiental y la conciencia humana. También priorizamos la aplicación de soluciones avanzadas y nuevos materiales para explorar la dirección futura de la arquitectura.

IDEE Architects

www.idee.vn

Trần Ngọc Linh
Nguyen Huy Hai

Ajisai Hill House

Kabuchin Penthouse

The house is situated on a steep mountain slope, overlooking a vast valley with a view of a golf course and the Tam Dao mountain range. The goal is seamless integration with the surrounding natural landscape. The space should accommodate an extended family with 5 bedrooms and additional auxiliary spaces.
The main house is constructed with a steel frame finished with stone and natural wood, sheltering the house from the impact of drastic weather conditions in the area. The use of wood and expansive awnings draws inspiration from traditional Vietnamese architectural spaces, featuring rows of columns and symmetrical spaces. The main traffic axis is centrally balanced between the house and the various open spaces, connecting the front yard to the rear. The spaces between the elevated levels gradually open up new vistas, linking with the project's backdrop.The garden and the roof of the garage block are connected, expanding the flower planting area.

Das Haus liegt an einem steilen Bergabhang und ist auf ein weites Tal mit Blick auf einen Golfplatz und die Tam Dao Gebirgskette ausgerichtet. Der Raum soll eine erweiterte Familie mit fünf Schlafzimmern und zusätzlichen Nebenräumen unterbringen. Das Haupthaus ist mit einem Stahlrahmen fertiggestellt, der mit Naturstein und Holz versehen ist und das Haus vor den Auswirkungen der drastischen Wetterbedingungen in der Region schützt. Die Verwendung von Holz und ausladenden Vordächern ist von traditionellen vietnamesischen architektonischen Räumen inspiriert, mit Reihen von Säulen und symmetrischen Räumen. Die Hauptverkehrsachse ist zentral zwischen dem Haus und den verschiedenen offenen Räumen ausbalanciert und verbindet die Vorder- mit der Rückseite des Hauses. Die Zwischenräume zwischen den Ebenen öffnen sich allmählich zu neuen Ausblicken und verbinden sich mit dem Hintergrund des Projekts. Der Garten und das Dach des Garagenblocks sind miteinander verbunden und erweitern die Blumenpflanzzone.

Ajisai Hill est située sur une pente de montagne abrupte, orientée vers une vaste vallée avec vue sur un terrain de golf et la chaîne de montagnes de Tam Dao. L'objectif est de s'intégrer parfaitement dans le paysage naturel environnant. L'espace doit accueillir une famille élargie avec cinq chambres et des espaces auxiliaires supplémentaires. La maison principale est construite avec un cadre en acier fini avec de la pierre et du bois naturel, protégeant la maison de l'impact des conditions climatiques drastiques de la région. L'utilisation de bois et de auvents expansifs s'inspire des espaces architecturaux traditionnels vietnamiens, avec des rangées de colonnes et des espaces symétriques. L'axe de circulation principal est équilibré au centre entre la maison et les divers espaces ouverts, reliant le patio avant à l'arrière. Les espaces entre les niveaux s'ouvrent progressivement sur de nouvelles vues, se liant au fond du projet. Le jardin et le toit du bloc de garage sont connectés, élargissant la zone de plantation de fleurs.

La casa está situada en una pendiente de montaña empinada, orientada a un amplio valle con vistas a un campo de golf y la cordillera de Tam Dao. El objetivo es integrarse perfectamente con el paisaje natural circundante. El espacio debe dar cabida a una familia extendida con cinco dormitorios y espacios auxiliares adicionales. La casa principal está construida con un marco de acero acabado con piedra y madera natural, protegiendo la casa del impacto de las condiciones climáticas drásticas en la zona. El uso de madera y toldos expansivos se inspira en los espacios arquitectónicos tradicionales vietnamitas, con filas de columnas y espacios simétricos. El eje de tráfico principal está equilibrado centralmente entre la casa y los diversos espacios abiertos, conectando el patio delantero con el trasero. Los espacios entre los niveles elevados gradualmente abren nuevas vistas, vinculándose con el fondo del proyecto. El jardín y el techo del bloque de garaje están conectados, ampliando la zona de plantación de flores.

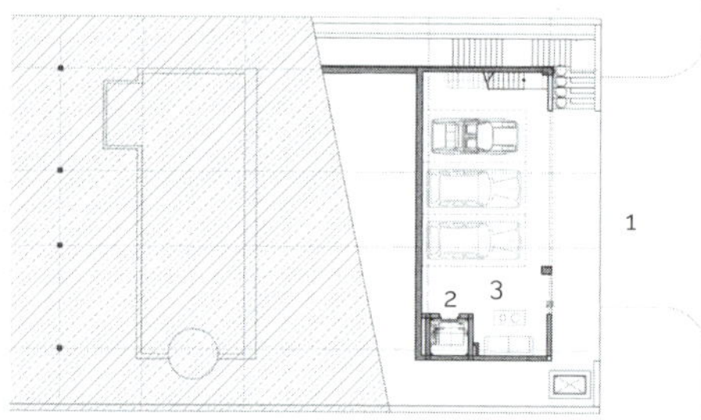

Ground floor plan

1. Entry
2. Elevator
3. Garage

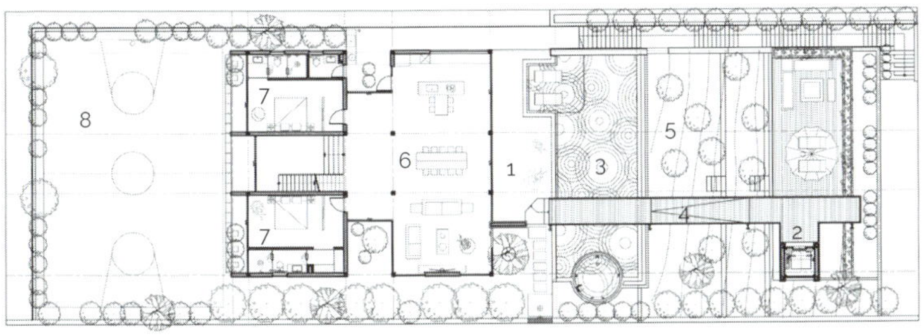

First floor plan

1. Entry
2. Elevator
3. Swimming Pool
4. Bridge
5. Ajisai Garden
6. Living Room
7. Bedroom

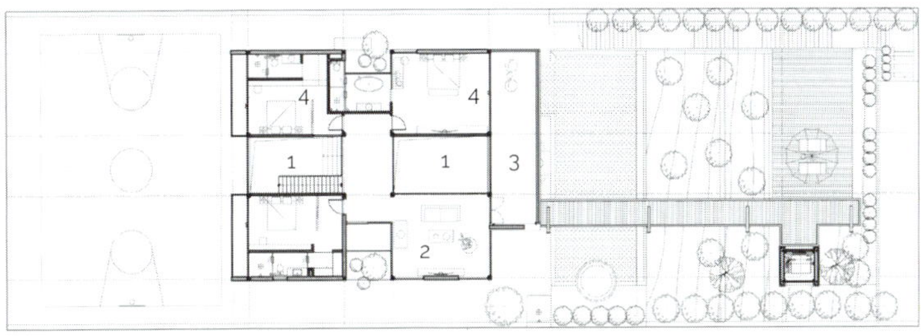

Second floor plan

1. Void
2. Living Romm
3. Terrace
4. Bedroom

Hà Nội, Vietnam // Photos © Triệu Chiến

The apartment, characterized by its soaring floor height, had become outdated, prompting the homeowner to undertake a substantial renovation due to the growing number of young family members. The architect envisioned creating a distinctive apartment with numerous play areas for children, such as a communal playground, while minimizing barriers between family members.
A large steel floor supported by a system of wooden columns was elevated to create a mezzanine for the children. In contrast, supplementary systems like sanitation, storage, and functional rooms were concealed within a large stone wall, interconnected by a thin steel floor. The communal space was expanded, eliminating partitions to merge seamlessly and offer panoramic views of the surroundings. Ancillary functions were concealed in recessed cabinets and rooms hidden within stone walls. Specific functions were organized into individual modules.

Die Wohnung, gekennzeichnet durch ihre hohe Deckenhöhe, war veraltet geworden, was den Besitzer veranlasste, aufgrund der wachsenden Anzahl junger Familienmitglieder eine umfassende Renovierung durchzuführen. Der Architekt stellte sich vor, eine markante Wohnung mit zahlreichen Spielbereichen für Kinder zu schaffen, während die Barrieren zwischen den Familienmitgliedern minimiert wurden. Ein großer Stahlboden, gestützt von einem System aus Holzsäulen, wurde angehoben, um eine Zwischendecke für die Kinder zu schaffen. Dazu waren ergänzende Systeme wie Sanitär, Lagerung und funktionale Räume innerhalb einer großen Steinmauer versteckt, die durch einen dünnen Stahlboden miteinander verbunden waren. Der gemeinschaftliche Raum wurde erweitert, indem Partitionen entfernt wurden, um nahtlos zu verschmelzen und einen Panoramablick auf die Umgebung zu bieten. Die Nebenfunktionen waren in Einbauschränken und verborgenen Räumen innerhalb von Steinmauern versteckt. Die spezifischen Funktionen waren in einzelnen Modulen angeordnet.

Kabuchin, caractérisé par sa hauteur de plafond élevée, était devenu obsolète, ce qui a poussé le propriétaire à entreprendre une rénovation en raison du nombre croissant de jeunes membres de la famille. L'architecte a imaginé créer un appartement distinctif avec de nombreuses aires de jeux pour enfants, telles qu'une aire de jeux communautaire, tout en minimisant les barrières entre les membres de la famille. Un grand plancher en acier soutenu par un système de colonnes en bois a été élevé pour créer une mezzanine pour les enfants. En revanche, les systèmes complémentaires tels que l'assainissement, le stockage et les pièces fonctionnelles étaient cachés à l'intérieur d'un grand mur de pierre, interconnectés par un plancher en acier mince. L'espace commun s'est agrandi, éliminant les cloisons pour fusionner sans problème et offrir des vues panoramiques sur l'environnement. Les fonctions auxiliaires étaient cachées dans des placards encastrés et des pièces cachées à l'intérieur de murs en pierre. Les fonctions spécifiques étaient organisées en modules individuels.

El apartamento, caracterizado por su altura de piso elevada, se había quedado obsoleto, lo que llevó al propietario a emprender una renovación debido al creciente número de miembros jóvenes de la familia. El arquitecto imaginó crear un apartamento con numerosas áreas de juego para niños, como un patio de recreo comunitario, mientras se minimizaban las barreras entre los miembros de la familia. Un gran piso de acero soportado por un sistema de columnas de madera se elevó para crear un entrepiso para los niños. En contraste, los sistemas complementarios como saneamiento, almacenamiento y habitaciones funcionales quedan ocultos dentro de un gran muro de piedra, interconectados por un piso de acero delgado. El espacio comunitario se expandió, eliminando particiones para fusionarse sin problemas y ofrecer vistas panorámicas del entorno. Las funciones auxiliares se ocultan en armarios empotrados y habitaciones escondidas dentro de muros de piedra. Las funciones específicas se organizaron en módulos individuales.

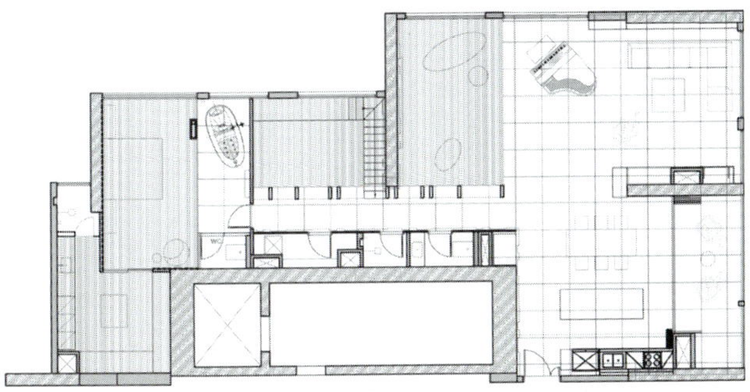

First floor plan

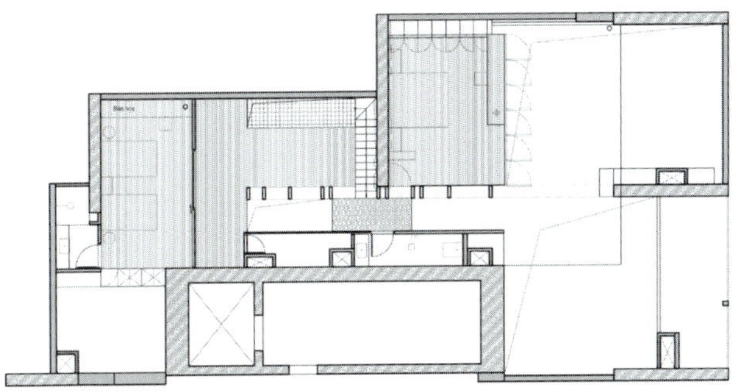

Second floor plan

Kaminsky Arkitektur is an award-winning firm founded in 2007 with 60 employees in offices in Gothenburg and Stockholm. The firm is dedicated to developing cutting-edge architecture and has positioned itself as an international benchmark for sustainable architecture and an active voice in contemporary debate.
Established in 2007 by Fredrik Kjellgren and Joakim Kaminsky as Kjellgren Kaminsky Arkitekter, the firm transitioned in 2021 when Fredrik departed. Today, Joakim Kaminsky continues the legacy leading the office.
Joakim Kaminsky has been awarded several prestigious scholarships, brings his expertise from roles at UN-Studio and Wingårdhs. He regularly teaches at Chalmers Architecture and has been a guest lecturer at architecture schools in Stockholm, Lund, Århus, and Trondheim.

Kaminsky Arkitektur ist ein preisgekröntes Unternehmen, das 2007 gegründet wurde und 60 Mitarbeiter in Büros in Göteborg und Stockholm beschäftigt. Das Büro widmet sich der Entwicklung modernster Architektur und hat sich als internationaler Maßstab für nachhaltige Architektur und als aktive Stimme in der zeitgenössischen Debatte positioniert.
Das Büro wurde 2007 von Fredrik Kjellgren und Joakim Kaminsky als Kjellgren Kaminsky Arkitekter gegründet und 2021 nach dem Ausscheiden von Fredrik Kaminsky umgewandelt. Heute führt Joakim Kaminsky das Erbe fort und leitet das Büro.
Joakim Kaminsky wurde mit mehreren renommierten Stipendien ausgezeichnet und bringt sein Fachwissen aus seiner Tätigkeit bei UN-Studio und Wingårdhs mit. Er unterrichtet regelmäßig an der Chalmers Architecture und war Gastdozent an Architekturschulen in Stockholm, Lund, Århus und Trondheim.

Kaminsky Arkitektur est un cabinet primé fondé en 2007 avec 60 employés répartis dans des bureaux à Göteborg et Stockholm. Le cabinet est dédié au développement d'une architecture de pointe et s'est positionné comme une référence internationale en matière d'architecture durable et comme une voix active dans le débat contemporain.
Établi en 2007 par Fredrik Kjellgren et Joakim Kaminsky en tant que Kjellgren Kaminsky Arkitekter, le cabinet a fait la transition en 2021 lorsque Fredrik est parti. Aujourd'hui, Joakim Kaminsky perpétue l'héritage en dirigeant le cabinet.
Joakim Kaminsky a reçu plusieurs bourses prestigieuses, apportant son expertise acquise chez UN-Studio et Wingårdhs. Il enseigne régulièrement à la Chalmers Architecture et a été conférencier invité dans des écoles d'architecture à Stockholm, Lund, Århus et Trondheim.

Kaminsky Arkitektur es una galardonada empresa fundada en 2007 con 60 empleados que trabajan en oficinas en Gotemburgo y Estocolmo. La firma se dedica a desarrollar arquitectura de vanguardia y se ha posicionado como un referente internacional de la arquitectura sostenible y una voz activa en el debate contemporáneo.
Fundada en 2007 por Fredrik Kjellgren y Joakim Kaminsky con el nombre de Kjellgren Kaminsky Arkitekter, la empresa pasó a llamarse Kjellgren Kaminsky Arkitekter en 2021, cuando Fredrik se marchó. Hoy, Joakim Kaminsky continúa el legado al frente del despacho.
Joakim Kaminsky ha recibido varias becas de prestigio y aporta su experiencia en UN-Studio y Wingårdhs. Imparte clases regularmente en Chalmers Architecture y ha sido profesor invitado en escuelas de arquitectura de Estocolmo, Lund, Århus y Trondheim.

Kaminsky Arkitektur

www.kaminsky.se

Kaminsky Arkitektur Team

Kristallen

Tyftet

In a forest on the outskirts of the city of Alingsås in Sweden, five climate-smart semi-detached houses are nestled harmoniously with the nature. The project incorporates a consistent focus on sustainability and a design with broken volumes strategically placed to complement the landscape. The houses are certified as passive houses according to FEBY Gold standards. They also hold the Nordic Swan eco-label. Constructed with a timber frame, the houses feature integrated solar panels on the roof. The position around a shared courtyard offers a great space for a playground and cultivation areas.

In einem Wald am Rande der Stadt Alingsås in Schweden schmiegen sich fünf klimagerechte Doppelhaushälften harmonisch in die Natur. Das Projekt beinhaltet einen konsequenten Fokus auf Nachhaltigkeit und ein Design mit gebrochenen Volumen, die strategisch platziert sind, um die Landschaft zu ergänzen.
Die Häuser sind als Passivhäuser nach dem FEBY-Gold-Standard zertifiziert. Außerdem tragen sie das Umweltzeichen Nordic Swan. Die Häuser sind in Holzrahmenbauweise errichtet und verfügen über integrierte Sonnenkollektoren auf dem Dach.
Die Lage um einen gemeinsamen Innenhof bietet viel Platz für einen Spielplatz und Anbauflächen.

Dans une forêt à la périphérie de la ville d'Alingsås en Suède, cinq maisons jumelées climatiquement intelligentes sont nichées harmonieusement dans la nature.
Le projet intègre un accent constant sur la durabilité et un design avec des volumes brisés stratégiquement placés pour compléter le paysage.
Les maisons sont certifiées passives selon les normes FEBY Gold. Elles portent également l'éco-label nordique Swan. Construites avec une ossature en bois, les maisons sont dotées de panneaux solaires intégrés sur le toit. La disposition autour d'une cour commune offre un grand espace pour une aire de jeux et des zones de culture.

En un bosque a las afueras de la ciudad sueca de Alingsås, cinco casas adosadas climáticamente inteligentes se asientan en armonía con la naturaleza. El proyecto incorpora una atención constante a la sostenibilidad y un diseño con volúmenes quebrados estratégicamente situados para complementar el paisaje.
Las casas están certificadas como «Casas Pasivas» según las normas FEBY Gold. También tienen la etiqueta ecológica Nordic Swan. Construidas con un armazón de madera, las casas cuentan con paneles solares integrados en el tejado. La posición en torno a un patio compartido ofrece un gran espacio para un parque infantil y zonas de cultivo.

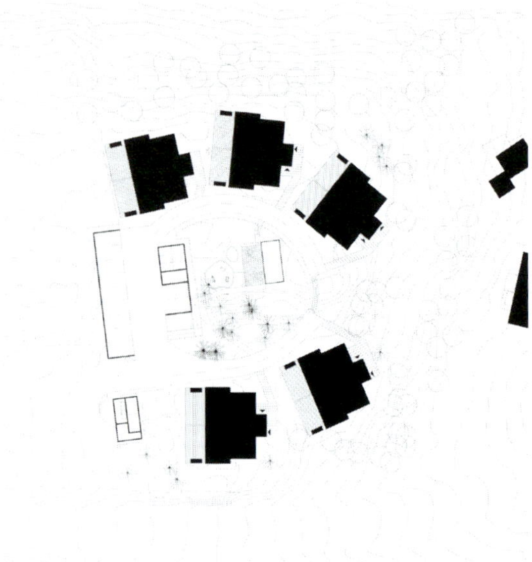

Site plan

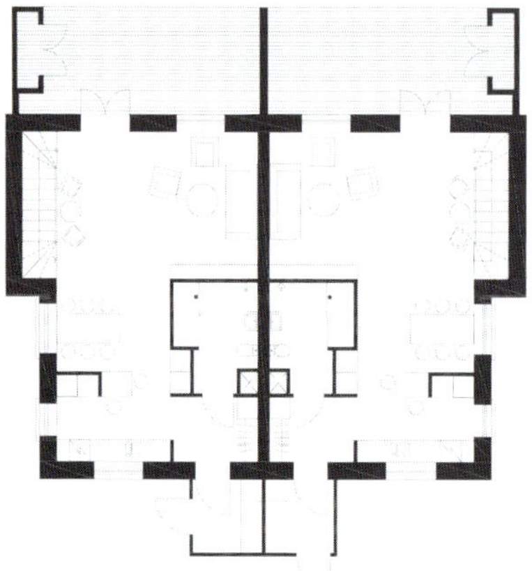

First floor plan

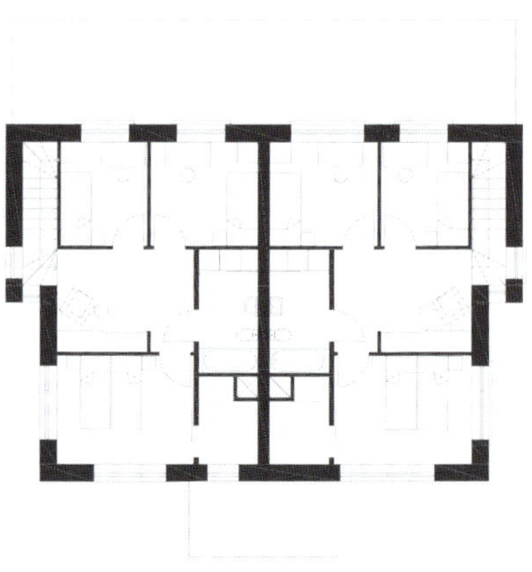

Second floor plan

Bollebygd, Sweden // Photos © Jan Töve

Seven semi-detached houses where the view towards the rolling meadows has been the setting for the project. The buildings are constructed in souterrain, with social areas placed towards the afternoon sun and the views, while bedrooms, storage spaces and technology are found on the ground floor.
The design has drawn inspiration from the local traditional architecture, but in an updated manner with standing wooden panels and gabled roofs in sinusoidal sheet metal. The facade color relates to the mellow tones of the landscape and contributes a low-key and responsive complement to the area's scenic location. The volumes are broken up by shifting each dwelling in relation to its neighbor. This way, the architecture feels less bulky and connects to the scale of the surrounding buildings.

Sieben Doppelhaushälften, bei denen der Blick auf die hügeligen Wiesen den Rahmen für das Projekt bildete. Die Gebäude sind in Souterrain-Bauweise errichtet, wobei die Sozialräume zur Nachmittagssonne und zur Aussicht hin ausgerichtet sind, während sich im Erdgeschoss Schlafzimmer, Abstellräume und Technik befinden.
Der Entwurf wurde von der traditionellen Architektur der Region inspiriert, jedoch auf moderne Weise mit stehenden Holzpaneelen und Giebeldächern aus sinusförmigem Blech. Die Farbe der Fassade nimmt Bezug auf die sanften Töne der Landschaft und ist eine zurückhaltende und ansprechende Ergänzung zur landschaftlichen Lage des Gebiets. Die Volumen werden durch die Verschiebung der einzelnen Häuser im Verhältnis zu ihren Nachbarn aufgelockert. Auf diese Weise wirkt die Architektur weniger wuchtig und fügt sich in den Maßstab der umliegenden Gebäude ein.

Sept maisons jumelées où la vue sur les prairies vallonnées a été le cadre du projet. Les bâtiments sont construits en souterrain, avec des espaces sociaux orientés vers le soleil de l'après-midi et la vue, tandis que les chambres, les espaces de rangement et la technologie se trouvent au rez-de-chaussée. Le design s'inspire de l'architecture traditionnelle locale, mais de manière mise à jour avec des panneaux de bois debout et des toits à pignon en tôle sinusoïdale. La couleur de la façade se rapporte aux tons doux du paysage et apporte un complément discret et réactif à l'emplacement pittoresque de la région. Les volumes sont brisés en déplaçant chaque logement par rapport à son voisin. Ainsi, l'architecture semble moins imposante et se connecte à l'échelle des bâtiments environnants.

Siete casas adosadas en las que la vista hacia los prados ondulados ha sido el escenario del proyecto. Los edificios están construidos en subterráneo, con las zonas sociales situadas hacia el sol de la tarde y las vistas, mientras que los dormitorios, los espacios de almacenamiento y la tecnología se encuentran en la planta baja.
El diseño se ha inspirado en la arquitectura tradicional local, pero de forma actualizada, con paneles de madera en pie y tejados a dos aguas de chapa sinusoidal. El color de la fachada guarda relación con los tonos suaves del paisaje y aporta un complemento discreto y sensible a la ubicación paisajística de la zona. Los volúmenes se rompen desplazando cada vivienda en relación con su vecina. De este modo, la arquitectura se siente menos voluminosa y conecta con la escala de los edificios circundantes.

Site plan

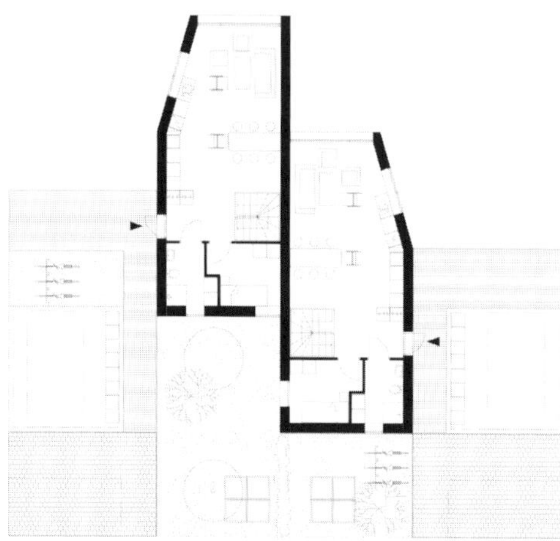

First floor plan

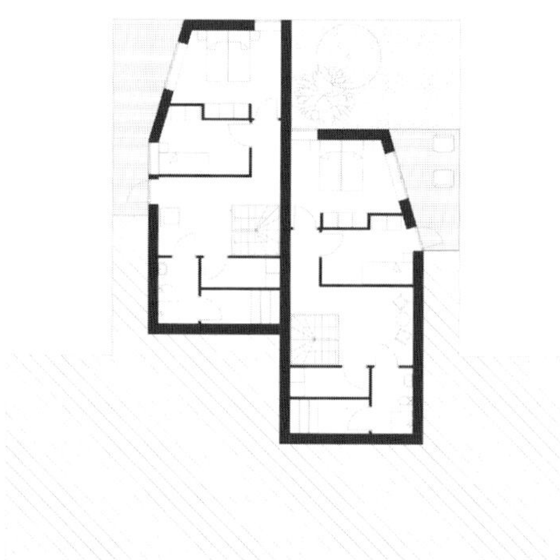

Second floor plan

Knut Hjeltnes was born in Drøbak, Norway in 1961, and was raised in Ås, a small university town south of Oslo. He studied at the Norwegian Institute of Technology in Trondheim from 1980-1986. During the latter half of his studies and for one and a half years after graduating he worked for 4B Architects. Since 1988 he has had his on practice. He taught at the Oslo school of Architecture from 1988-2016, the last 12 years as professor. He has lectured in several countries, been awarded several prizes and his work is widely published.
The practice was established in Oslo as a one-man practice, slowly expanding to its current size of six employees. The office concentrate on houses, weekend homes and smaller public works. In a period over several years in the 1990s he cooperated with Haga and Grov Architects in Stavanger.

Knut Hjeltnes wurde 1961 in Drøbak, Norwegen, geboren und wuchs in Ås, einer kleinen Universit.tsstadt südlich von Oslo, auf. Er studierte von 1980 bis 1986 am Norwegischen Institut für Technologie in Trondheim. Während der zweiten Hälfte seines Studiums und eineinhalb Jahre
nach seinem Abschluss arbeitete er für 4B Architects. Seit 1988 hat er sein eigenes Büro. Von 1988 bis 2016 unterrichtete er an der Oslo School of Architecture, die letzten 12 Jahre als Professor. Er hat in mehreren Ländern Vorlesungen gehalten, wurde mit mehreren Preisen ausgezeichnet, und seine Arbeiten werden vielfach veröffentlicht. Das Büro wurde in Oslo als Ein-Mann-Praxis gegründet, die sich langsam auf ihre derzeitige Größe von sechs Mitarbeitern ausweitete. Das Büro konzentriert sich auf Häuser, Wochenendhäuser und kleinere öffentliche Arbeiten. In den 1990er Jahren arbeitete er über mehrere Jahre hinweg mit Haga and Grov Architects in Stavanger zusammen.

Knut Hjeltnes est né à Drøbak, en Norvège, en 1961, et a grandi à Ås, une petite ville universitaire au sud d'Oslo. Il a étudié à l'Institut norvégien de technologie de Trondheim de 1980 à 1986. Pendant la seconde moitié de ses études et pendant un an et demi après l'obtention de son diplôme, il a travaillé pour 4B Architects. Depuis 1988, il a son propre cabinet. Il a enseigné à l'école d'architecture d'Oslo de 1988 à 2016, les 12 dernières années en tant que professeur. Il a donné des conférences dans plusieurs pays, a reçu plusieurs prix et ses travaux sont largement publiés.
Le cabinet a été créé à Oslo en tant que cabinet unipersonnel et s'est lentement développé pour atteindre sa taille actuelle de six employés. Le bureau se concentre sur les maisons, les résidences secondaires et les petits travaux publics. Dans les années 1990, il a coopéré pendant plusieurs années avec Haga and Grov Architects à Stavanger.

Knut Hjeltnes nació en Drøbak, Noruega, en 1961, y se crió en Ås, una pequeña ciudad universitaria al sur de Oslo. Estudió en el Instituto Noruego de Tecnología en Trondheim de 1980 a 1986. Durante la última mitad de sus estudios y durante un año y medio después de graduarse trabajó para 4B Architects. Desde 1988 ha tenido su propio estudio. Enseñó en la Escuela de Arquitectura de Oslo de 1988 a 2016, los últimos 12 años como profesor. Ha dado conferencias en varios países, ha recibido varios premios y su trabajo es ampliamente publicado.
El estudio se estableció en Oslo como un estudio de un solo hombre, expandiéndose lentamente hasta su tamaño actual de seis empleados. La oficina se concentra en el diseño de casas, casas de fin de semana y pequeñas obras públicas. En un periodo de varios años en la década de 1990 cooperó con Haga and Grov Architects en Stavanger.

Knut Hjeltnes

www.hjeltnes.as

Knut Hjeltnes Team

Cabin Hjeltnes

Cabin Ersland

Hårsøy, Norway // Photos © Knut Hjeltnes

This small summerhouse is built on a roadless island out in the southernmost archipelago of Norway. An important intention was to erect a low cost holiday home with minimal ecological impact both as construction and in the subsequent use. The cabin is in use from April to October and is completely shut down during winter. Transportation to and fro the island is by sail, oars or electric propulsion dependant on wind and weather. From the pier it is a 200m walk along a path to the small settlement.
The plot is located at the center of the small island on a meadow, at the edge of a little forest, the views are of greenery, tree trunks and walls of bare rock. Despite a location only 100m from the sea, the sea is just barely glimpsed from the site.
The program is divided in three separate buildings, a main cabin, an annex and a shed. All three buildings share the same general concept but nuances occur according to their different uses.

Dieses kleine Sommerhaus wurde auf einer straßenlosen Insel in den südlichsten Schären Norwegens gebaut. Ein wichtiges Ziel war es, ein kostengünstiges Ferienhaus mit minimalen ökologischen Auswirkungen sowohl beim Bau als auch bei der späteren Nutzung zu errichten. Die Hütte ist von April bis Oktober in Betrieb und wird im Winter komplett stillgelegt. Der Transport zur und von der Insel erfolgt je nach Wind und Wetter mit Segel, Ruder oder Elektroantrieb. Von der Anlegestelle sind es 200 m Fußweg bis zur kleinen Siedlung. Das Grundstück liegt in der Mitte der kleinen Insel auf einer Wiese, am Rande eines kleinen Waldes, mit Blick auf Grünflächen, Baumstämme und nackte Felswände. Trotz der Lage nur 100 m vom Meer entfernt, ist das Meer vom Grundstück aus kaum zu erahnen. Das Programm ist in drei separate Gebäude unterteilt, ein Hauptgebäude, ein Nebengebäude und ein Schuppen. Alle drei Gebäude haben das gleiche allgemeine Konzept, aber je nach ihrer unterschiedlichen Nutzung gibt es Nuancen.

Cette petite maison d'été est construite sur une île sans route, dans l'archipel le plus méridional de Norvège. L'intention principale était de construire une maison de vacances à faible coût avec un impact écologique minimal, tant pendant la construction que dans son utilisation ultérieure. La cabine est utilisée d'avril à octobre et est complètement fermée en hiver. Le transport vers et depuis l'île se fait en voile, à la rame ou avec une propulsion électrique selon le vent et la météo. Depuis le quai, il faut marcher 200 mètres le long d'un sentier jusqu'au petit village. La parcelle est située au centre de la petite île, dans une prairie, à l'orée d'une petite forêt. Les vues sont composées de verdure, de troncs d'arbres et de parois de roches nues. Malgré une situation à seulement 100 mètres de la mer, la mer n'est qu'aperçue depuis le site. Le programme est divisé en trois bâtiments distincts : une cabine principale, une annexe et une remise. Les trois bâtiments partagent le même concept général mais des nuances apparaissent en fonction de leurs utilisations respectives.

Esta pequeña casa de verano está construida en una isla sin carreteras del archipiélago más meridional de Noruega. La intención inicial consistía en erigir una casa de vacaciones de bajo coste con un impacto ecológico mínimo tanto en su construcción como en su uso posterior. La cabaña se utiliza de abril a octubre y se cierra por completo en invierno. El transporte hacia y desde la isla se realiza a vela, remos o propulsión eléctrica, dependiendo del viento y el tiempo. Desde el embarcadero hay un paseo de 200 m por un sendero hasta el pequeño asentamiento.
La parcela está situada en el centro de la pequeña isla en un prado, en el borde de un pequeño bosque, donde las vistas son de vegetación, troncos de árboles y paredes de roca desnuda. A pesar de estar situado a sólo 100 m del mar, éste apenas se vislumbra desde el solar.
El programa se divide en tres edificios separados, una cabaña principal, un anexo y un cobertizo. Los tres edificios comparten el mismo concepto general, pero se producen matices en función de sus diferentes usos.

Landøy, Norway // Photos © Francesca Iarrusso, Knut Hjeltnes

The cabin was conceived as a kind of outfarm for the family's cabin a few hundred meters away. As it has turned out, they prefer the new cabin, so the use is now the opposite. Is located high above the sea with a fantastic view towards the skerries and the horizon.
The cabin is constructed as a skeleton of glue-lam beams and post and the roof is of massive wood construction, in the main rooms raised as pyramids. The pyramids are painted on the inside, each in a different colour. The open air living room has large shutters that can be opened and closed due to wind, sun or wanted views.

Die Hütte war als eine Art Vorwerk für die nur wenige hundert Meter entfernte Hütte der Familie gedacht. Wie sich herausgestellt hat, ziehen sie die neue Hütte vor, so dass die Nutzung nun umgekehrt ist. Sie liegt hoch über dem Meer mit einem fantastischen Blick auf die Schären und den Horizont.
Die Hütte ist als Skelett aus Leimbindern und Pfosten gebaut und das Dach ist eine massive Holzkonstruktion, in den Haupträumen als Pyramiden aufgeständert. Die Pyramiden sind auf der Innenseite jeweils in einer anderen Farbe gestrichen.
Das Freiluftwohnzimmer hat große Fensterläden, die je nach Wind, Sonne oder gewünschter Aussicht geöffnet und geschlossen werden können.

La cabine a été conçue comme une sorte de dépendance de la cabine familiale située à quelques centaines de mètres. Comme il s'est avéré, ils préfèrent maintenant la nouvelle cabine, alors l'utilisation est désormais inverse. Elle est située en hauteur au-dessus de la mer avec une vue fantastique sur les écueils et l'horizon. La cabine est construite comme un squelette de poutres en lamellé-collé et de poteaux, et le toit est construit en bois massif, dans les pièces principales élevées comme des pyramides. Les pyramides sont peintes à l'intérieur, chacune dans une couleur différente. Le salon extérieur a de grandes persiennes qui peuvent être ouvertes et fermées en fonction du vent, du soleil ou des vues souhaitées.

La cabaña se concibió como una especie de dependencia de la cabaña familiar situada a unos cientos de metros. Resultó que los propietarios preferían la nueva cabaña, así que ahora el uso es el contrario. Está situada en lo alto, sobre el mar, con una vista fantástica hacia los Skerries y el horizonte.
La cabaña está construida como un esqueleto de vigas y postes de madera encolada y el tejado es de madera maciza, en las habitaciones principales levantadas como pirámides pintadas por dentro, cada una de un color diferente.
El salón al aire libre tiene grandes contraventanas que pueden abrirse y cerrarse en función del viento, el sol o las vistas deseadas.

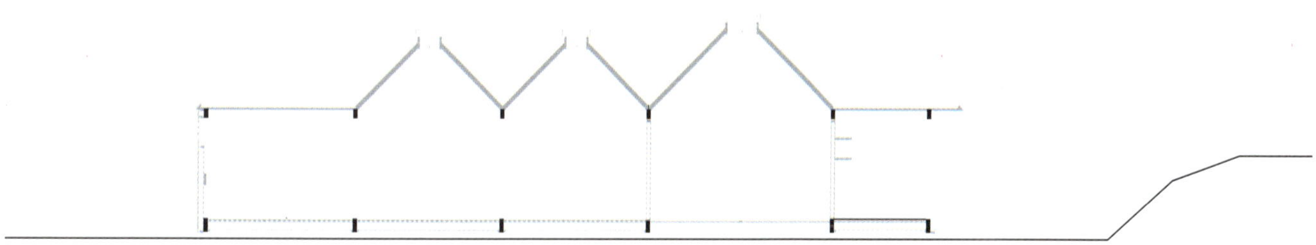

Section

Our architect design office is based in Kyoto, Japan. We incorporate beautiful and delicate touch rooted in the city and culture of Kyoto into our designs. We work with clients not only in Japan but overseas clients. Our main work includes, but not limited to, residences, interior-design, hotel/restaurant design, and store/shop design. We create the most unique space that is different from common design that is suitable for the space. Please experience our beautiful and delicate attention we provide just like the Omo-te-nashi/hospitality of Kyoto.

Unser Architekturbüro befindet sich in Kyoto, Japan. In unsere Entwürfe fließen die Schönheit und das Feingefühl ein, die in der Stadt und der Kultur von Kyoto verwurzelt sind. Wir arbeiten nicht nur mit Kunden in Japan, sondern auch mit Kunden in Übersee. Unsere Haupttätigkeit umfasst unter anderem Wohnhäuser, Innenarchitektur, Hotel-/Restaurantdesign und Laden-/Geschäftsdesign. Wir schaffen einzigartige Räume, die sich vom üblichen Design unterscheiden und für den jeweiligen Raum geeignet sind. Erleben Sie unsere schöne und delikate Aufmerksamkeit, die wir wie die Omo-te-nashi/Gastfreundschaft von Kyoto bieten.

Notre bureau d'architecture est basé à Kyoto, au Japon. Nous incorporons une touche belle et délicate enracinée dans la ville et la culture de Kyoto dans nos conceptions. Nous travaillons avec des clients non seulement au Japon mais aussi à l'étranger. Notre travail principal comprend, mais ne se limite pas à, des résidences, du design d'intérieur, du design d'hôtel/restaurant et du design de magasin/boutique. Nous créons l'espace le plus unique qui diffère du design commun adapté à l'espace. Veuillez faire l'expérience de notre attention belle et délicate que nous offrons, tout comme l'Omo-te-nashi/l'hospitalité de Kyoto.

Nuestro estudio de diseño arquitectónico tiene su sede en Kioto, Japón. Incorporamos a nuestros diseños toques bellos y delicados arraigados en la ciudad y la cultura de la ciudad. Trabajamos con clientes no sólo en Japón, sino también en el extranjero. Nuestro trabajo principal incluye, entre otros, residencias, diseño de interiores, diseño de hoteles/restaurantes y diseño de tiendas/comercios. Creamos el espacio más único, diferente del diseño común que es adecuado para el espacio. Experimente nuestra hermosa y delicada atención que proporcionamos al igual que el Omo-te-nashi/hospitalidad de Kyoto.

Koyori

www.koyori-n2.com

Nahoko Nakamura,
Masahiko Nakamura

Leafmania Yoyogi Uehara

House in Kitatoryo Area

Tokyo, Japan // Photos © Junichi Usui

The venue occupies the 1st and 2nd floors of the "CABO" complex, a multifaceted facility for work, residence, and recreation that emerged in 2023. The 1st floor currently functions as a gallery primarily showcasing the works of craft artists. The space is modern and minimal, with natural light and artificial lighting create a source of illumination that introduces vibrations, incorporating materials such as stainless steel, *Kurotani washi* (Japanese paper), and a floor finished with deep grass washing. The 2nd floor houses a tea house. It incorporates classical elements. Maximizing openings, it introduces soft light into the space through shoji screens adorned with Kurotani washi. Constructed solely with materials that encapsulate light and present soft expressions, the design aims to convey a serene world where patrons can calmly engage with the Chinese tea provided by the owner.

Der Veranstaltungsort befindet sich im 1. und 2. Stock des „CABO"-Komplexes, einer vielseitigen Einrichtung zum Arbeiten, Wohnen und Erholen, die im Jahr 2023 entstand. Die erste Etage dient derzeit als Galerie, in der vor allem die Werke von Kunsthandwerkern ausgestellt werden. Der Raum ist modern und minimalistisch, mit natürlichem und künstlichem Licht, das eine Lichtquelle schafft, die Vibrationen erzeugt, und mit Materialien wie rostfreiem Stahl, *Kurotani-Washi* (japanisches Papier) und einem Boden, der mit tiefem Gras gewaschen ist. Im 2. Stock befindet sich ein Teehaus. Es enthält klassische Elemente. Durch die Maximierung der Öffnungen wird sanftes Licht durch die mit Kurotani-Washi verzierten Shoji-Schirme in den Raum geleitet. Das Design besteht ausschließlich aus Materialien, die das Licht einfangen und einen sanften Ausdruck vermitteln, und zielt darauf ab, eine heitere Welt zu schaffen, in der die Gäste in aller Ruhe den chinesischen Tee genießen können, den der Besitzer anbietet.

L'emplacement occupe les 1er et 2e étages du complexe « CABO », une installation polyvalente pour le travail, la résidence et les loisirs qui a émergé en 2023. Le 1er étage fonctionne actuellement comme une galerie présentant principalement les œuvres d'artistes artisans. L'espace est moderne et minimaliste, avec une lumière naturelle et artificielle créant une source d'illumination introduisant des vibrations, incorporant des matériaux tels que l'acier inoxydable, le *Kurotani washi* (papier japonais) et un sol fini avec un lavage d'herbe profonde. Le 2e étage abrite une maison de thé. Il intègre des éléments classiques. Maximisant les ouvertures, il introduit une lumière douce dans l'espace à travers des cloisons shoji ornées de Kurotani washi. Construit uniquement avec des matériaux qui encapsulent la lumière et présentent des expressions douces, le design vise à transmettre un monde serein où les clients peuvent s'engager calmement avec le thé chinois fourni par le propriétaire.

El local ocupa las plantas 1ª y 2ª del complejo «CABO», una instalación polifacética para el trabajo, la residencia y el ocio que surgió en 2023. La 1ª planta funciona actualmente como galería, donde se exponen principalmente obras de artistas artesanos. El espacio es moderno y minimalista, con luz natural e iluminación artificial que crean una fuente de iluminación que introduce vibraciones, incorporando materiales como acero inoxidable, *Kurotani washi* (papel japonés) y un suelo acabado con un profundo lavado de hierba. La 2ª planta alberga una casa de té. El proyecto incorpora elementos clásicos. Aprovechando al máximo las aberturas, introduce una suave luz en el espacio a través de pantallas shoji adornadas con Kurotani washi. Construido únicamente con materiales que encapsulan la luz y presentan expresiones suaves, el diseño pretende transmitir un mundo sereno en el que los clientes puedan disfrutar tranquilamente del té chino que ofrece el propietario.

Kyoto, Japan // Photos © Junichi Usui

The following is the concept for the renovation of the traditional Kyoto townhouse that I designed.
It is a renovation project of a 116-year-old townhouse built in the 40th year of the Meiji era.
While preserving the traditional appearance of a Kyoto townhouse, the interior was reconfigured to combine Japanese aesthetics with a contemporary layout. Additionally, special attention was given to the compact yet characteristic townhouse courtyard, reevaluating its connection with the interior environment and rebuilding it accordingly.
The layout was designed to allow a visual connection from the entrance to the back garden. Throughout each floor and room, traditional plaster finishes and materials such as Kyoto's Kurotani washi paper were used to harmonize with the traditional atmosphere of a Kyoto townhouse. Frost glass and shoji screens were incorporated into the windows to envelop the space in soft light.

Im Folgenden wird das von mir entworfene Konzept für die Renovierung eines traditionellen Kyotoer Stadthauses vorgestellt.
Es handelt sich um ein Renovierungsprojekt für ein 116 Jahre altes Stadthaus, das im 40. Jahr der Meiji-Ära erbaut wurde.
Während das traditionelle Erscheinungsbild eines Kyotoer Stadthauses beibehalten wurde, wurde das Innere neu gestaltet, um japanische Ästhetik mit einem modernen Layout zu verbinden. Besonderes Augenmerk wurde dabei auf den kompakten, aber charakteristischen Innenhof des Stadthauses gelegt, dessen Verbindung mit dem Innenraum neu bewertet und entsprechend umgestaltet wurde. In jedem Stockwerk und jedem Raum wurden traditionelle Putzoberflächen und Materialien wie das Kurotani-Washi-Papier aus Kyoto verwendet, um mit der traditionellen Atmosphäre eines Kyotoer Stadthauses zu harmonieren. Frostglas und Shoji-Scheiben wurden in die Fenster integriert, um den Raum in weiches Licht zu hüllen.

Voici le concept pour la rénovation de la maison traditionnelle de Kyoto que j'ai conçue. Il s'agit d'un projet de rénovation d'une maison de ville vieille de 116 ans construite à l'époque de la 40e année de l'ère Meiji. Tout en préservant l'aspect traditionnel d'une maison de ville de Kyoto, l'intérieur a été reconfiguré pour combiner l'esthétique japonaise avec une disposition contemporaine. De plus, une attention particulière a été accordée à la cour de la maison compacte mais caractéristique, réévaluant sa connexion avec l'environnement intérieur et la reconstruisant en conséquence.
La disposition a été conçue pour permettre une connexion visuelle de l'entrée au jardin arrière. À chaque étage et dans chaque pièce, des finitions traditionnelles en plâtre et des matériaux tels que le papier Kurotani de Kyoto ont été utilisés pour s'harmoniser avec l'atmosphère traditionnelle d'une maison de Kyoto. Des vitres givrées et des cloisons shoji ont été incorporées dans les fenêtres pour envelopper l'espace d'une lumière douce.

A continuación se presenta el concepto de renovación de la casa tradicional de Kioto.
Se trata de un proyecto de renovación de una casa adosada de 116 años de antigüedad construida en el año 40 de la era Meiji.
Aunque se conservó el aspecto tradicional de una casa de Kioto, el interior se reconfiguró para combinar la estética japonesa con un diseño contemporáneo. Además, se prestó especial atención al compacto pero característico patio de la casa, reevaluando su conexión con el entorno interior y reconstruyéndolo en consecuencia. La distribución se diseñó para permitir una conexión visual desde la entrada hasta el jardín trasero. En todas las plantas y habitaciones se utilizaron acabados tradicionales de yeso y materiales como el papel washi Kurotani de Kioto para armonizar con el ambiente tradicional de una casa adosada de Kioto. En las ventanas se incorporaron cristales esmerilados y pantallas shoji para envolver el espacio en una luz suave.

Lazor/Office, founded in 2003 by Charlie Lazor, is a design practice committed to creating buildings and spaces that enhance peoples' lives. We place primacy on place-making, a sensitive, integrated approach to organizing and synthesizing a client's program and preferences on the site—an approach that fosters a profound connection with nature, light, and climate. We value what has come before and look to a region's historical structures for cues and clues to guide our new contribution to the landscape. Collaboration with our client's is essential to producing successful buildings. We begin by listening and then continue to listen to understand fully how our clients want to live and work. At the same time, we observe the surrounding environment—the land, the sun, the stars, the sounds. By applying both our expertise and our imagination, we achieve architecture that seamlessly hosts the occupants, frames the natural world outside, and delights the senses.

Lazor/Office, gegründet im Jahr 2003 von Charlie Lazor, ist ein Designstudio, das sich der Schaffung von Gebäuden und Räumen verschrieben hat, die das Leben der Menschen verbessern. Wir legen Wert auf die Schaffung von Orten, einen sensiblen und integrierten Ansatz, um das Programm und die Vorlieben eines Kunden in Bezug auf den Ort zu organisieren und zu synthetisieren, einen Ansatz, der eine tiefe Verbindung zur Natur, zum Licht und zum Klima fördert. Wir schätzen das, was zuvor geschehen ist, und suchen in den historischen Strukturen einer Region nach Signalen und Hinweisen, um unseren neuen Beitrag zur Landschaft zu führen. Die Zusammenarbeit mit unseren Kunden ist entscheidend für erfolgreiche Gebäude. Wir beginnen mit dem Zuhören und hören weiterhin zu, um vollständig zu verstehen, wie unsere Kunden leben und arbeiten möchten. Gleichzeitig beobachten wir die umgebende Umgebung: das Land, die Sonne, die Sterne, die Geräusche. Durch die Anwendung sowohl unserer Erfahrung als auch unserer Vorstellungskraft erreichen wir eine Architektur, die die Bewohner perfekt beherbergt, die natürliche Umgebung außerhalb des Gebäudes umrahmt und die Sinne erfreut.

Lazor/Office, fondé en 2003 par Charlie Lazor, est un cabinet de design engagé dans la création de bâtiments et d'espaces visant à améliorer la vie des personnes. Nous accordons une priorité à la création de lieux, adoptant une approche sensible et intégrée pour organiser et synthétiser le programme et les préférences d'un client concernant le lieu. Cette approche encourage une connexion profonde avec la nature, la lumière et le climat. Nous valorisons le passé et recherchons des signaux et des indices dans les structures historiques d'une région pour guider notre nouvelle contribution au paysage. La collaboration avec nos clients est essentielle pour créer des bâtiments réussis. Nous commençons par écouter et continuons à écouter pour comprendre pleinement comment nos clients veulent vivre et travailler. En même temps, nous observons l'environnement : la terre, le soleil, les étoiles, les sons. En appliquant à la fois notre expérience et notre imagination, nous parvenons à une architecture qui accueille parfaitement les occupants, encadre le monde naturel extérieur et ravit les sens.

Lazor/Office, fundada en 2003 por Charlie Lazor, es un estudio de diseño comprometido con la creación de edificios y espacios que mejoren la vida de las personas. Damos primacía a la creación de lugares, un enfoque sensible e integrado para organizar y sintetizar el programa y las preferencias de un cliente en cuanto al lugar, un enfoque que fomenta una conexión profunda con la naturaleza, la luz y el clima. Valoramos lo que ha ocurrido antes y buscamos en las estructuras históricas de una región señales y pistas para guiar nuestra nueva contribución al paisaje. La colaboración con nuestros clientes es esencial para producir edificios exitosos. Comenzamos escuchando y continuamos escuchando para comprender completamente cómo nuestros clientes quieren vivir y trabajar. Al mismo tiempo, observamos el entorno circundante: la tierra, el sol, las estrellas, los sonidos. Al aplicar tanto nuestra experiencia como nuestra imaginación, logramos una arquitectura que aloja perfectamente a los ocupantes, enmarca el mundo natural exterior y deleita los sentidos.

Lazor/ Office

www.lazoroffice.com

Charlie Lazor

Peek-a-Boo Cabin

New Auburn, Wisconsin, USA // Photos © Jasper Lazor Photography

Rising on steel legs above a glacially formed landscape, the Peek-a-Boo Cabin faces a large lake. A series of transitional spaces—exterior stairs, a deck, an open breezeway—are carved into the clean, horizontal box form, nurturing a symbiotic relationship between structure, site and occupants. On arrival, an exterior stairway leads through a deep entry portal revealing the water and forest. The private areas of domesticity are rendered as minimalist box forms, captured between roof and floor. The spaces between them create a "peek-a-boo" experience; deep-framed views of lake and woods. The "box" bedrooms and baths, day lit by a single window and red box surround, act as a deep frame onto an intimately scaled view, befitting a personal space. A breezeway with outdoor shower provides passage to the children's bunkhouse, set in the tree canopy. A raw, basalt stone wall—a remnant of a local farmer's walls—courses through the shared kitchen-living-dining space, punctuated by a fireplace.

Die Kabine Peek-a-Boo, die sich auf Stelzen aus Stahl über einer glazial geformten Landschaft erhebt, blickt auf einen großen See. Eine Reihe von Übergangsräumen wie Außentreppen, eine Terrasse und ein offener Flur sind in Form einer sauberen, horizontalen Box geschnitzt und fördern eine symbiotische Beziehung zwischen der Struktur, dem Gelände und den Bewohnern. Eine Außentreppe durch ein tiefes Eingangstor, das Wasser und den Wald enthüllt. Die privaten Bereiche der Hauswirtschaft sind als minimalistische Kistenformen dargestellt. Die Räume zwischen ihnen „spionieren" die tiefen Ausblicke auf den See und den Wald aus. Die Schlafzimmer und Badezimmer, die durch Tageslicht durch ein einzelnes Fenster beleuchtet und von roten Kisten umgeben sind, wirken als tiefer Rahmen für einen intimen, für einen persönlichen Raum geeigneten Blick. Ein Flur mit einer Außendusche führt zum Kinder-Etagenhaus, das sich in der Baumkrone befindet. Eine Mauer aus rohem Basaltgestein, durchzieht den gemeinsamen Raum von Küche-Wohnzimmer-Esszimmer und wird von einem Kamin unterbrochen.

Peek-a-Boo, s'élevant sur des pattes en acier au-dessus d'un paysage façonné par les glaciers, regarde vers un grand lac. Une série d'espaces de transition, tels que des escaliers extérieurs, une terrasse et un couloir ouvert, sont sculptés dans la forme d'une boîte propre et horizontale, favorisant une relation symbiotique entre la structure, le terrain et les occupants. Un escalier extérieur mène à travers un portail d'entrée profond qui révèle l'eau et la forêt. Les zones privées de domesticité sont représentées comme des formes de boîtes minimalistes, capturées entre le toit et le sol. Les espaces entre elles « espionnent » les vues profondes sur le lac et la forêt. Les chambres et salles de bains, éclairées par la lumière du jour à travers une seule fenêtre et entourées de boîtes rouges, agissent comme un cadre profond pour une vue d'échelle intime, adaptée à un espace personnel. Un couloir avec une douche extérieure donne accès à la maison de couchettes pour enfants, située dans la cime des arbres. Un mur de basalte brut, traverse l'espace partagé de la cuisine-salle de séjour-salle à manger, interrompu par une cheminée.

Elevándose sobre patas de acero sobre un paisaje formado glacialmente, la Cabaña Peek-a-Boo mira hacia un gran lago. Una serie de espacios de transición, como escaleras exteriores, una terraza y un pasillo abierto, están tallados en forma de caja limpia y horizontal, fomentando una relación simbiótica entre la estructura, el terreno y los ocupantes. Una escalera exterior conduce a través de un portal de entrada profundo que revela el agua y el bosque. Las áreas privadas de domesticidad se representan como formas de caja minimalistas, capturadas entre el techo y el suelo. Los espacios entre ellas «espían» las vistas profundas del lago y el bosque. Los dormitorios y baños, iluminados por la luz del día a través de una sola ventana y rodeados de cajas rojas, actúan como un marco profundo para una vista de escala íntima. Un pasillo con ducha al aire libre proporciona paso a la casa de literas para niños, ubicada en la copa de los árboles. Un muro de piedra basáltica cruda, atraviesa el espacio compartido de cocina-sala de estar-comedor, interrumpido por una chimenea.

Floor plan

1. Outdoor Room 1
2. Kitchen
3. Lounge
4. Bedroom
5. Desk Niche
6. Bedroom
7. Outdoor Room 2
8. Bedroom Pod
9. Bedroom Pod
10. Outdoor Shower
11. Bedroom
12. Bath
13. Dining
14. Bathroom
15. Bedroom
16. The Shed

We develop unique and mindful architectural projects that focus on the ever changing interaction between man and nature. Our office is based in Tamarindo, Guanacaste, Costa Rica. We built our company in 2006. Since then, we have been exploring techniques, materials, environments and disciplines. Our international and local experience gives us a wide perspective when approaching a project. We take enough time to understand and interpret our clients needs and desires. We work hand in hand with our clients, architects, designers, engineers, builders, accountants and environmentalists. We love to introduce new ways of thinking our projects. That´s why we call ourselves a "laboratory." We are constantly combining structures, materials and perspectives in the entire process. We take care of the world in which we live. Before looking further, we look around us. We prefer local materials, techniques and manpower.

Wir entwickeln einzigartige und bewusste architektonische Projekte, die sich auf die sich ständig verändernde Interaktion zwischen Mensch und Natur konzentrieren. Unser Büro befindet sich in Tamarindo, Guanacaste, Costa Rica. Wir haben unser Unternehmen im Jahr 2006 gegründet. Seitdem haben wir Techniken, Materialien, Umgebungen und Disziplinen erkundet. Unsere internationale und lokale Erfahrung gibt uns eine breite Perspektive, wenn wir ein Projekt angehen. Wir nehmen uns Zeit, um die Bedürfnisse und Wünsche unserer Kunden zu verstehen und zu interpretieren. Wir arbeiten Hand in Hand mit unseren Kunden, Architekten, Designern, Ingenieuren, Bauunternehmern, Wirtschaftsprüfern und Umweltschützern. Wir lieben es, neue Denkansätze in unsere Projekte einzubringen. Deshalb nennen wir uns ein „Labor." Während des gesamten Prozesses kombinieren wir ständig Strukturen, Materialien und Perspektiven. Wir sorgen uns um die Welt, in der wir leben. Bevor wir nach mehr suchen, schauen wir uns um. Wir bevorzugen lokale Materialien, Techniken und Verarbeitung.

Nous développons des projets architecturaux uniques et conscients qui se concentrent sur l'interaction en constante évolution entre l'homme et la nature. Notre bureau est situé à Tamarindo, Guanacaste, Costa Rica. Nous avons créé notre entreprise en 2006. Depuis lors, nous avons exploré des techniques, des matériaux, des environnements et des disciplines. Notre expérience internationale et locale nous permet d'avoir une large perspective lorsque nous abordons un projet. Nous prenons le temps de comprendre et d'interpréter les besoins et les désirs de nos clients. Nous travaillons main dans la main avec nos clients, architectes, designers, ingénieurs, constructeurs, comptables et écologistes. Nous aimons introduire de nouvelles façons de penser dans nos projets. C'est pourquoi nous nous qualifions de « laboratoire ». Nous combinons constamment les structures, les matériaux et les perspectives tout au long du processus. Nous nous soucions du monde dans lequel nous vivons. Avant de chercher plus, nous regardons autour de nous. Nous préférons les matériaux, les techniques et la main-d'œuvre locaux.

Desarrollamos proyectos arquitectónicos únicos y conscientes que se centran en la interacción siempre cambiante entre el hombre y la naturaleza. Nuestra oficina se encuentra en Tamarindo, Guanacaste, Costa Rica. Construimos nuestra empresa en 2006. Desde entonces, hemos estado explorando técnicas, materiales, ambientes y disciplinas. Nuestra experiencia internacional y local nos da una amplia perspectiva al abordar un proyecto. Nos tomamos el tiempo suficiente para entender e interpretar las necesidades y deseos de nuestros clientes. Trabajamos mano a mano con nuestros clientes, arquitectos, diseñadores, ingenieros, constructores, contables y ecologistas. Nos encanta introducir nuevas formas de pensar en nuestros proyectos. Por eso nos llamamos «laboratorio». Combinamos constantemente estructuras, materiales y perspectivas en todo el proceso. Cuidamos el mundo en el que vivimos. Antes de buscar más, miramos a nuestro alrededor. Preferimos los materiales, las técnicas y la mano de obra locales.

LSD Architects

www.lsd.cr

Rodolfo Tinocco
Luis Mauricio Solís

Casa Ondas

Placed in a small terrace in the mountains of Playa Tamarindo with amazing ocean views, we found Casa Ondas. It was conceptualized as an elongated structure, positioned in an existent terrace, with two main volumes separated by an open but covered terrace, dividing Social from Private areas. The house was designed in multiple levels for a better use of the existent terrace and sloped areas around it. Four independents and very particular roofs, overlaps on top of the social and private areas, unifying the program of the house and bringing a lot of light in between the roof, creating a unique space for the social areas. Steel columns support the roofs with just a few lower walls, creating very big opening to the views and bringing a lot of natural light into the spaces and the elongated shape of the house improves natural cross ventilation through all the house. This house was created with the intention of increasing the interaction of the interior and exterior space, so that the user can truly experience life in the tropics.

Auf einer kleinen Terrasse in den Bergen von Playa Tamarindo mit herrlichem Blick auf das Meer befindet sich Casa Ondas. Es wurde als langgestreckte Struktur konzipiert, die in einer bestehenden Terrasse positioniert ist, mit zwei Hauptvolumina, die durch eine offene, aber überdachte Terrasse getrennt sind, die den Sozialbereich vom Privatbereich trennt. Das Haus wurde auf mehreren Ebenen entworfen, um die vorhandene Terrasse und die schrägen Bereiche um sie herum besser nutzen zu können. Vier unabhängige und sehr spezielle Dächer, die sich über den sozialen und privaten Bereichen überlappen, vereinen das Programm des Hauses und lassen viel Licht zwischen den Dächern herein, wodurch ein einzigartiger Raum für die sozialen Bereiche entsteht. Stahlsäulen stützen die Dächer mit nur wenigen niedrigeren Wänden, wodurch eine sehr große Öffnung für die Aussicht geschaffen wird und viel natürliches Licht in die Räume gelangt, und die längliche Form des Hauses verbessert die natürliche Querlüftung im ganzen Haus.

Située dans les montagnes de Playa Tamarindo, avec une vue imprenable sur la mer, se trouve la Casa Ondas. Elle a été conçue comme une structure allongée, positionnée sur une terrasse existante, avec deux volumes principaux séparés par une terrasse ouverte mais couverte, séparant les zones sociales des zones privées. La maison a été conçue sur plusieurs niveaux afin d'utiliser au mieux la terrasse existante et les zones en pente qui l'entourent. Quatre toits indépendants et très particuliers se chevauchent au sommet, unifiant le programme de la maison et apportant beaucoup de lumière entre les toits, créant un espace unique pour les parties communes. Des colonnes en acier soutiennent les plafonds avec seulement quelques murs en dessous, créant de grandes ouvertures vers les vues et permettant à la lumière naturelle de pénétrer dans les espaces. La forme allongée de la maison favorise la ventilation transversale naturelle. Cette maison a été créée dans le but d'accroître l'interaction entre l'espace intérieur et l'espace extérieur.

Ubicada en una pequeña terraza en las montañas de Playa Tamarindo con impresionantes vistas al mar, encontramos Casa Ondas. Fue conceptualizada como una estructura alargada, posicionada en una terraza existente, con dos volúmenes principales separados por una terraza abierta pero cubierta, dividiendo las áreas sociales de las privadas. La casa fue diseñada en múltiples niveles para un mejor uso de la terraza existente y las áreas inclinadas que la rodean. Cuatro techos independientes y muy particulares se superponen en la parte superior, unificando el programa de la casa y proporcionando mucha luz entre los techos, creando un espacio único para las áreas comunes. Columnas de acero sostienen los techos con solo unas pocas paredes inferiores, creando grandes aberturas hacia las vistas y permitiendo que mucha luz natural entre en los espacios. La forma alargada de la casa mejora la ventilación natural cruzada. Esta casa fue creada con la intención de aumentar la interacción entre el espacio interior y exterior.

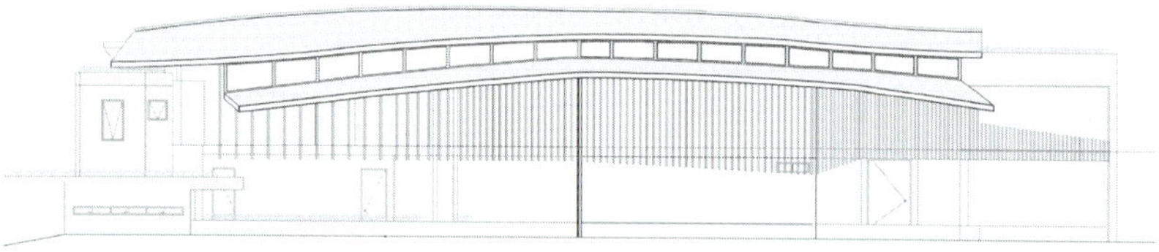

East elevation

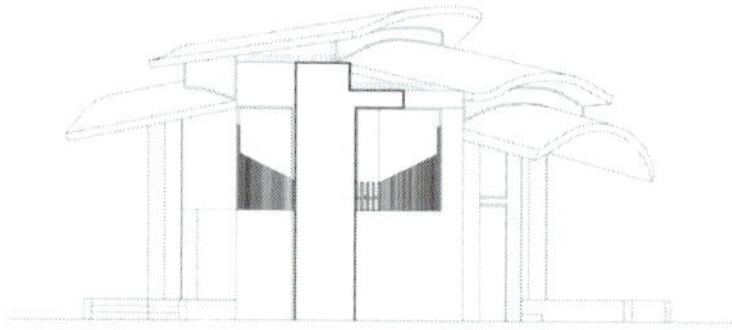

North elevation

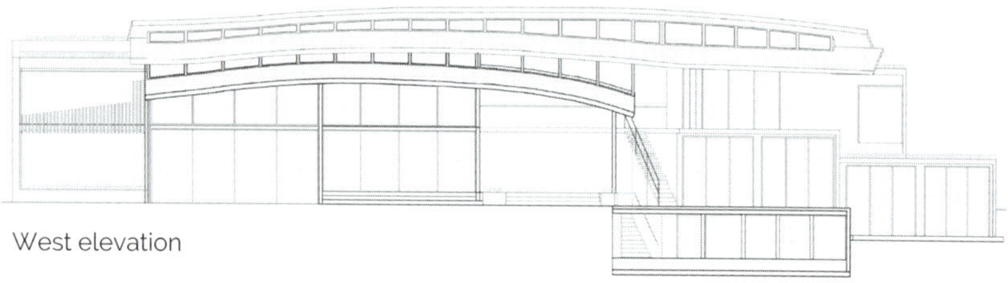

West elevation

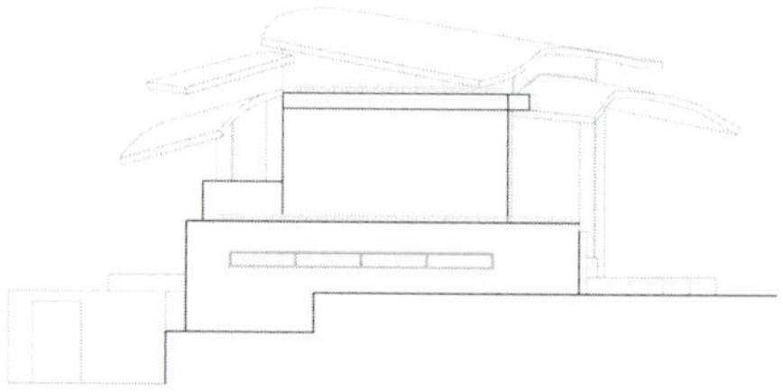

South elevation

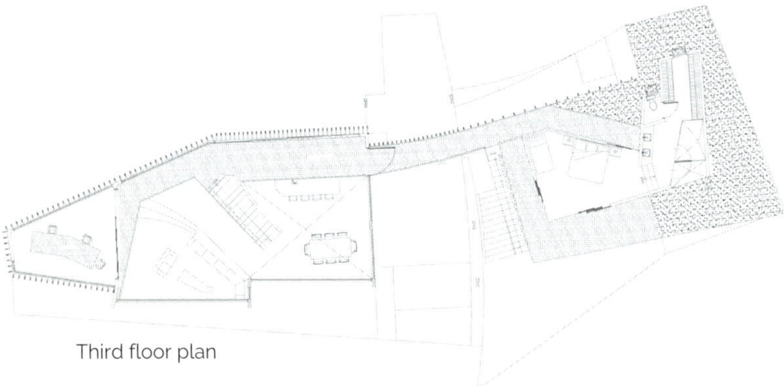

Third floor plan

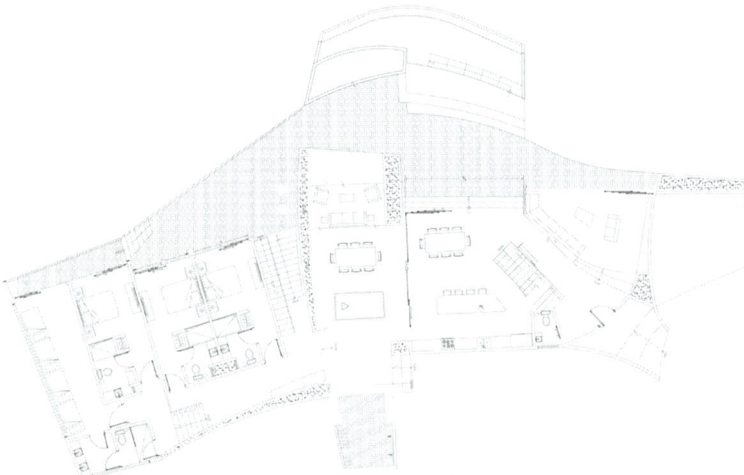

Second floor plan

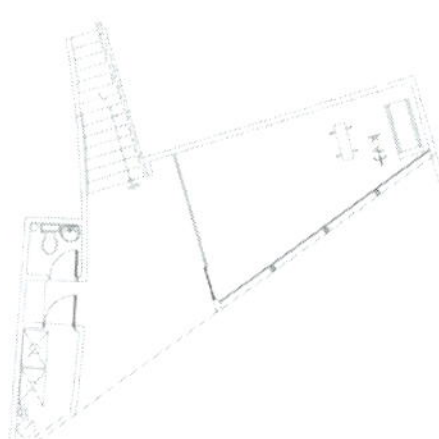

First floor plan

Maryann Thompson Architects is an award-winning Boston area firm known for architecture which is sustainable, regionally driven, and which connects the built environment to the natural world. The firm's staff comes from diverse backgrounds, including architecture, landscape architecture, planning, interior design and the visual arts. Maryann has degrees in both architecture and landscape architecture, and brings to the practice a respect for an interdisciplinary approach to design where issues of the environment and landscape are central to our design thinking. We believe in the potential for architecture to engage the human subject through a heightening of the awareness of the phenomenological qualities of the site. Our attempt is to reinforce the "genius loci" of a site through the creation of an architecture that is locally specific.

Maryann Thompson Architects ist ein preisgekröntes Unternehmen aus der Bostoner Gegend, das für seine nachhaltige, regional orientierte Architektur bekannt ist, die die gebaute Umgebung mit der natürlichen Welt verbindet. Das Team des Unternehmens stammt aus verschiedenen Bereichen wie Architektur, Landschaftsgestaltung, Stadtplanung, Innenarchitektur und bildenden Künsten. Maryann hat Abschlüsse in Architektur und Landschaftsgestaltung und bringt ihre Wertschätzung für einen interdisziplinären Designansatz in das Studio ein, bei dem Umweltfragen und Landschaftsgestaltung eine zentrale Rolle spielen. Wir glauben an das Potenzial der Architektur, den Menschen durch ein tieferes Bewusstsein für die phänomenologischen Qualitäten des Ortes einzubeziehen. Wir versuchen, den „genius loci" eines Ortes durch die Schaffung einer lokalspezifischen Architektur zu stärken.

Maryann Thompson Architects est une entreprise primée basée dans la région de Boston, connue pour son architecture durable, orientée vers la région et connectant le cadre bâti au monde naturel. Le personnel de l'entreprise provient de divers domaines tels que l'architecture, l'aménagement paysager, la planification, la conception d'intérieur et les arts visuels. Maryann est diplômée en architecture et en aménagement paysager, et apporte au studio son respect pour une approche interdisciplinaire de la conception dans laquelle les questions environnementales et paysagères occupent une place centrale. Nous croyons au potentiel de l'architecture pour engager l'être humain grâce à une conscience accrue des qualités phénoménologiques du site. Nous essayons de renforcer le « genius loci » d'un lieu en créant une architecture spécifique au lieu.

Maryann Thompson Architects es una galardonada empresa de la zona de Boston conocida por su arquitectura sostenible, orientada a la región y que conecta el entorno construido con el mundo natural. El personal de la empresa procede de diversos campos, como la arquitectura, el paisajismo, la planificación, el diseño de interiores y las artes visuales. Maryann es licenciada en arquitectura y paisajismo, y aporta al estudio su respeto por un enfoque interdisciplinar del diseño en el que las cuestiones medioambientales y paisajísticas ocupan un lugar central. Creemos en el potencial de la arquitectura para implicar al ser humano a través de una mayor conciencia de las cualidades fenomenológicas del sitio. Intentamos reforzar el «genius loci» de un lugar mediante la creación de una arquitectura localmente especifica.

Maryann Thompson Architects

www.maryannthompson.com

Maryann Thompson

Polly Hill Arboretum

Martha's Vineyard, Massachusetts, USA // Photos © Jeremy Bitterman, Chuck Choi

The new visitor center were designed as simple shed forms which heighten the visitor's relationship to the site. Outdoors, the complex layering of trellis, heavy timber frame, and perforated planes of the roofs mediate the natural light as do the trees above them.
Architectural elements such as a window seat and skylight expand the interior volume out past the building's heavy timber perimeter frame, pushing the interior into the surrounding natural site. Frosted glass, slatted walls, extensive clerestory windows, and skylights all reinforce the parallels of the visual and physical experience of the interior with the experience of the forest's interior on the other side of the walls. The skylight allows for the quality of light that one finds within the forest canopy. The wooden buildings are heavy timber Douglas fir construction, reminiscent of the old barns of New England.

Das neue Besucherzentrum wurde als einfache Schuppen gestaltet, die die Beziehung des Besuchers zum Ort verbessern. Außen strukturieren ein komplexes Gitterwerk aus Fensterläden, schwere Holzkonstruktionen und durchbrochene Dächer das natürliche Licht, ebenso wie die Bäume, die über ihnen aufragen. Architektonische Elemente wie ein Fenstersitz und ein Oberlicht erweitern das Innenvolumen über die schwere Holzumrandung des Gebäudes hinaus und drängen das Innere in die umgebende Naturlandschaft. Mattglas, Lamellenwände, große Oberlichter und Oberlichter verstärken die Parallelität zwischen der visuellen und physischen Erfahrung des Innenraums und der Erfahrung des Waldinnenraums jenseits der Mauern. Das Oberlicht ermöglicht es, die Lichtqualität im Blätterdach des Waldes zu genießen. Die Gebäude bestehen aus schwerem Douglasienholz und erinnern an alte Scheunen in Neuengland.

Le nouveau centre d'accueil a été conçu comme de simples hangars qui renforcent la relation du visiteur avec le lieu. À l'extérieur, le complexe de treillis, la structure lourde en bois et les toits perforés médient avec la lumière naturelle, tout comme les arbres qui s'élèvent au-dessus d'eux. Des éléments architecturaux tels qu'un siège de fenêtre et un puits de lumière élargissent le volume intérieur au-delà de la structure périphérique lourde en bois du bâtiment, poussant l'intérieur vers le paysage naturel environnant. Le verre dépoli, les murs en lames, les grandes lucarnes et les puits de lumière renforcent le parallélisme entre l'expérience visuelle et physique de l'intérieur et l'expérience de l'intérieur de la forêt de l'autre côté des murs. Le puits de lumière permet de profiter de la qualité de la lumière trouvée dans la canopée de la forêt. Les bâtiments sont en bois massif de sapin Douglas, rappelant les vieux granges de la Nouvelle-Angleterre.

El nuevo centro de visitantes se diseñó como simples cobertizos que realzan la relación del visitante con el lugar. En el exterior, el complejo entramado de celosías, la pesada estructura de madera y los planos perforados de los tejados median con la luz natural, al igual que los árboles que se alzan sobre ellos.
Elementos arquitectónicos como un asiento en la ventana y una claraboya amplían el volumen interior más allá de la pesada estructura perimetral de madera del edificio, empujando el interior hacia el paraje natural circundante. El vidrio esmerilado, las paredes de lamas, las amplias ventanas cenitales y las claraboyas refuerzan el paralelismo entre la experiencia visual y física del interior y la experiencia del interior del bosque al otro lado de los muros. La claraboya permite disfrutar de la calidad de luz que se encuentra en el dosel del bosque. Los edificios son de madera pesada de abeto Douglas, que recuerda a los viejos graneros de Nueva Inglaterra.

Emiliano Ruidiaz Riffo is an Architect from the University of Chile in 2015, graduated in Housing and City Policies from the Catholic University of Chile in 2020, and with undergraduate studies at the Università degli Studi Roma Tre, Italy. In 2019, he founded the office Medio Arquitectura, based in the city of Villarrica, in the south of Chile. The office focuses on achieving high standards of design, efficiency and sustainability in all phases and stages of the project, prioritising the use of wood as the main material. The most important thing for Medio Arquitectura is the experience of the people who will inhabit the place, seeking to contribute to their physical and emotional well-being, using architecture as a means to this end.

Emiliano Ruidiaz Riffo schloss 2015 sein Architekturstudium an der Universität von Chile ab und absolvierte 2020 ein Studium der Wohnungs- und Stadtpolitik an der Katholischen Universität von Chile sowie ein Grundstudium an der Università degli Studi Roma Tre, Italien. Im Jahr 2019 gründete er das Büro Medio Arquitectura mit Sitz in der Stadt Villarrica im Süden von Chile. Das Büro konzentriert sich darauf, hohe Standards in Bezug auf Design, Effizienz und Nachhaltigkeit in allen Phasen und Stadien des Projekts zu erreichen, wobei die Verwendung von Holz als Hauptmaterial im Vordergrund steht. Das Wichtigste für Medio Arquitectura ist die Erfahrung der Menschen, die den Ort bewohnen werden, und das Bestreben, zu ihrem physischen und emotionalen Wohlbefinden beizutragen, wobei die Architektur als Mittel zu diesem Zweck eingesetzt wird.

Emiliano Ruidiaz Riffo est architecte de l'Université du Chili en 2015, diplômé en logement et en politiques urbaines de l'Université catholique du Chili en 2020, et avec des études de premier cycle à l'Université degli Studi Roma Tre, en Italie. En 2019, il a fondé le bureau Medio Arquitectura, basé dans la ville de Villarrica, dans le sud du Chili. Le bureau se concentre sur l'atteinte de normes élevées en matière de conception, d'efficacité et de durabilité dans toutes les phases et étapes du projet, en donnant la priorité à l'utilisation du bois comme matériau principal. La chose la plus importante pour Medio Arquitectura est l'expérience des personnes qui habiteront le lieu, cherchant à contribuer à leur bien-être physique et émotionnel, en utilisant l'architecture comme moyen pour atteindre cet objectif.

Emiliano Ruidiaz Riffo es Arquitecto de la Universidad de Chile en 2015, diplomado en Políticas de Vivienda y Ciudad de la Universidad Católica de Chile en 2020, y con estudios de pre-grado en la Università degli Studi Roma Tre, Italia. En 2019, funda la oficina Medio Arquitectura, con sede en la ciudad de Villarrica, en el sur de Chile. La oficina se centra en alcanzar elevados estándares de diseño, eficiencia y sostenibilidad en todas las fases y etapas del proyecto, priorizando el uso de la madera como material principal. Lo más importante para Medio Arquitectura es la experiencia de las personas que habitarán el lugar, buscando aportar a su bienestar físico y emocional, utilizando la arquitectura como un medio para esto.

Medio Arquitectura

www.medioarquitectura.com

Emiliano Ruidiaz Riffo

Casa Tekila

Refugio Hachi

Lican Ray, Chile // Photos © Emiliano Ruidíaz Riffo

Casa Tekila is a house located in the south of Chile, in the Araucania region, a few kilometres from the town of Lican Ray. The main requirement was to design an efficient, comfortable, well-lit house with a good view of the lake. The project site has the Calafquen lake to the south and native forest to the north. The main decision was to raise the project from ground level with two objectives; the first, to seek the northern sun allowing the greatest entry of light and heat, and the second, to obtain a better view of the lake. The terrace of the project is projected to the south to contemplate the lake and to be protected from the summer sun. The main space; dining room, living room and kitchen, is positioned in an east-west direction, thus achieving a view of the lake and the forest.

Casa Tekila ist ein Haus im Süden Chiles, in der Region Araucania, nur wenige Kilometer von der Stadt Lican Ray entfernt. Die Hauptanforderung bestand darin, ein effizientes, komfortables und lichtdurchflutetes Haus mit einem guten Blick auf den See zu entwerfen. Das Grundstück grenzt im Süden an den Calafquen-See und im Norden an den Urwald. Die wichtigste Entscheidung war, das Projekt vom Boden aus anzuheben, und zwar mit zwei Zielen: erstens, um die nördliche Sonne zu nutzen und so den größten Lichteinfall und die größte Wärme zu erhalten, und zweitens, um einen besseren Blick auf den See zu bekommen. Die Terrasse des Projekts ist nach Süden ausgerichtet, um den See zu betrachten und vor der Sommersonne geschützt zu sein. Der Hauptraum - Esszimmer, Wohnzimmer und Küche - ist in Ost-West-Richtung ausgerichtet, um einen Blick auf den See und den Wald zu ermöglichen.

Casa Tekila est une maison située dans le sud du Chili, dans la région d'Araucania, à quelques kilomètres de la ville de Lican Ray. La principale exigence était de concevoir une maison efficace, confortable, bien éclairée avec une bonne vue sur le lac. Le site du projet a le lac Calafquen au sud et la forêt native au nord. La principale décision a été de surélever le projet du sol avec deux objectifs ; le premier, de rechercher le soleil du nord permettant la plus grande entrée de lumière et de chaleur, et le second, d'obtenir une meilleure vue sur le lac. La terrasse du projet est projetée vers le sud pour contempler le lac et être protégée du soleil estival. L'espace principal ; salle à manger, salon et cuisine, est positionné dans une direction est-ouest, réalisant ainsi une vue sur le lac et la forêt.

Casa Tekila es una vivienda ubicada en el sur de Chile, región de la Araucanía, a pocos kilómetros del pueblo de Lican Ray. El principal requerimiento era diseñar una vivienda eficiente, cómoda, iluminada y con buena vista al lago. El emplazamiento del proyecto tiene el lago Calafquen hacia el sur y bosque nativo hacia el norte. La decisión principal fue levantar al proyecto del nivel de suelo con dos objetivos; el primero, buscar el sol norte permitiendo la mayor entrada de luz y calor, y el segundo, obtener una mejor vista al lago. La terraza se proyecta hacia el sur para contemplar el lago y protegerse del sol de verano. El espacio principal; comedor, living y cocina, se posiciona en sentido oriente-poniente, de esta forma logra tener vista hacia el lago y hacia el bosque.

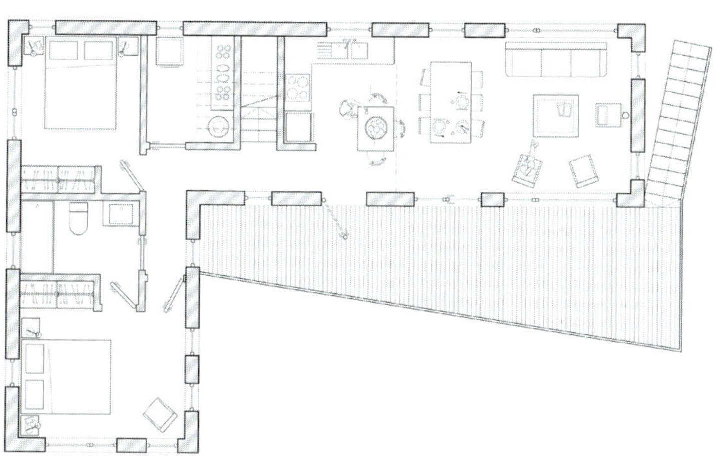

First floor plan

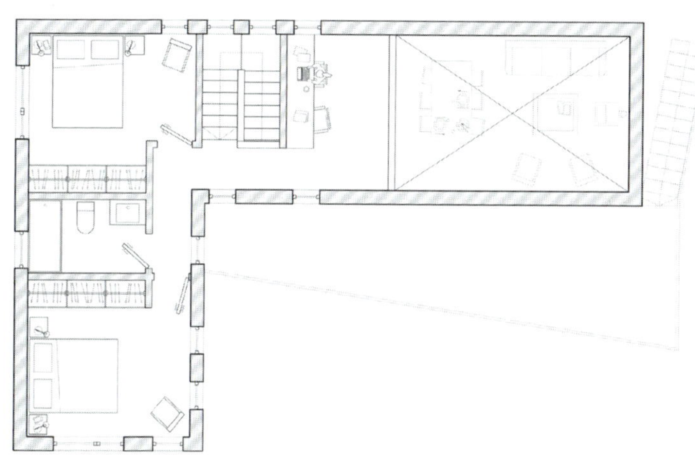

Second floor plan

Villarrica, Chile // Photos © Emiliano Ruidíaz Riffo

Refugio Hachi is a project located in the rural area of the commune of Villarrica, southern Chile. It is situated on a plot of land with abundant native forest and, with the aim of preserving the existing trees and making the most of the light and heat, it was decided to locate the project in the only clearing available. The client, a goldsmith and jeweller, wanted a refuge that would not only be her home, but also a place to design and work. The design of this space had to meet the following requirements: thermally efficient, comfortable, spacious, light and with a view of the native forest. Being a project of few square meters, it was decided to design a single large space, dispensing with dividing walls and using slopes to mark the difference between rooms.

Refugio Hachi ist ein Projekt in der ländlichen Gegend der Gemeinde Villarrica im Süden Chiles. Es befindet sich auf einem Grundstück mit reichlich einheimischem Wald, und mit dem Ziel, die vorhandenen Bäume zu erhalten und das Licht und die Wärme optimal zu nutzen, wurde beschlossen, das Projekt auf der einzigen verfügbaren Lichtung zu errichten. Die Bauherrin, eine Goldschmiedin und Juwelierin, wollte ein Refugium, das nicht nur ihr Zuhause sein sollte, sondern auch ein Ort zum Entwerfen und Arbeiten. Die Gestaltung dieses Raums musste folgende Anforderungen erfüllen: thermisch effizient, komfortabel, geräumig, hell und mit Blick auf den heimischen Wald. Da es sich um ein Projekt mit nur wenigen Quadratmetern handelt, wurde beschlossen, einen einzigen großen Raum zu entwerfen, auf Trennwände zu verzichten und den Unterschied zwischen den Räumen durch Schrägen zu markieren.

Refugio Hachi est un projet situé dans la zone rurale de la commune de Villarrica, au sud du Chili. Il est situé sur un terrain avec une abondante forêt native et, dans le but de préserver les arbres existants et de profiter au maximum de la lumière et de la chaleur, il a été décidé de situer le projet dans la seule clairière disponible. Le client, un bijoutier et joaillier, voulait un refuge qui ne serait pas seulement sa maison, mais aussi un endroit pour concevoir et travailler. La conception de cet espace devait répondre aux exigences suivantes : thermiquement efficace, confortable, spacieux, lumineux et avec une vue sur la forêt native. Étant un projet de quelques mètres carrés, il a été décidé de concevoir un seul grand espace, en dispensant des murs de division et en utilisant des pentes pour marquer la différence entre les pièces.

Refugio Hachi es un proyecto ubicado en el área rural de la comuna de Villarrica, sur de Chile. Se sitúa en un terreno con abundante bosque nativo y, con el objetivo de preservar los arboles existentes y aprovechar al máximo la luz y calor, se decidió ubicar el proyecto en el único claro disponible. La clienta, una orfebre joyera, quería un refugio que no solo fuera su hogar, sino al mismo tiempo un lugar para diseñar y trabajar. El diseño de este espacio debía cumplir los siguientes requisitos: eficiente térmicamente, cómodo, amplio, iluminado y con vista al bosque nativo. Al ser un proyecto de pocos metros cuadrados, se optó por diseñar un solo gran espacio, prescindiendo de muros divisorios y utilizando desniveles para marcar la diferencia entre recintos.

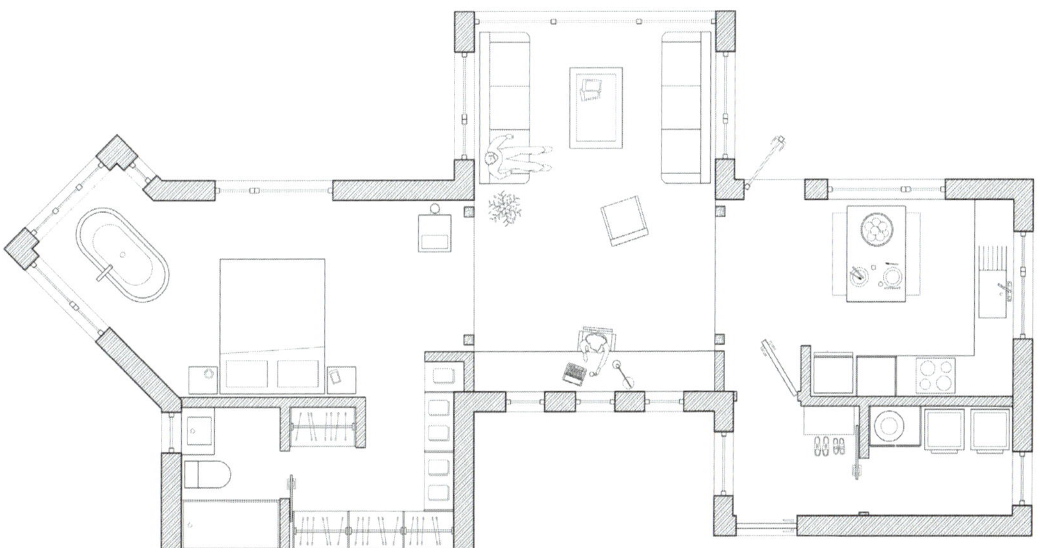

Ground floor plan

Nicole Blair is an architect and general contractor working in Austin, Texas, the city where she was born and raised. Her practice focuses on residential, small commercial, and public art building projects. Nicole's design approach is client and context driven, striving to find novel solutions that are closely tailored to her client's needs and personal style. In 2019 Elle Decor named Nicole one of the greatest living architects in the world, alongside several Pritzker Prize winners. Her projects have received numerous design awards – local to international – and her work has been published in books, magazines, and ad campaigns worldwide. She gained early work experience in the NYC offices of Robert A.M. Stern and Peter Eisenman architects and obtained a Bachelor of Science in Textiles and Apparel from Cornell and a Master of Architecture from Rice.

Nicole Blair ist eine Architektin und Generalunternehmerin, die in Austin, Texas, arbeitet, der Stadt, in der sie geboren und aufgewachsen ist. Ihr Fokus liegt auf Wohnbau, kleinen Gewerbeimmobilien und öffentlicher Kunst. Nicoles Designansatz basiert auf dem Kunden und dem Kontext und sucht nach innovativen Lösungen, die eng an die Bedürfnisse und den persönlichen Stil ihrer Kunden angepasst sind. 2019 ernannte Elle Decor Nicole zu einer der bedeutendsten lebenden Architektinnen der Welt, neben mehreren Pritzker-Preisträgern. Ihre Projekte wurden mit zahlreichen Designpreisen, sowohl lokal als auch international, ausgezeichnet, und ihre Arbeit wurde in Büchern, Zeitschriften und Werbekampagnen auf der ganzen Welt veröffentlicht. Sie sammelte frühzeitig Berufserfahrung in den New Yorker Büros der Architekten Robert A.M. Stern und Peter Eisenman und erwarb einen Bachelor of Science in Textilien und Bekleidung an der Cornell University sowie einen Master in Architektur an der Rice University.

Nicole Blair est une architecte et entrepreneuse générale travaillant à Austin, au Texas, la ville où elle est née et a grandi. Son studio se concentre sur des projets de construction résidentielle, de petits commerces et d'art public. L'approche de conception de Nicole est basée sur le client et le contexte, cherchant des solutions novatrices qui s'adaptent étroitement aux besoins et au style personnel de ses clients. En 2019, Elle Decor a nommé Nicole l'une des plus grandes architectes vivantes au monde, aux côtés de plusieurs lauréats du Prix Pritzker. Ses projets ont reçu de nombreux prix de design, tant locaux qu'internationaux, et son travail a été publié dans des livres, des magazines et des campagnes publicitaires à travers le monde. Elle a acquis une expérience professionnelle précoce dans les bureaux new-yorkais des architectes Robert A.M. Stern et Peter Eisenman, et a obtenu un baccalauréat ès sciences en textiles et confection de l'Université Cornell et une maîtrise en architecture de l'Université Rice.

Nicole Blair es una arquitecta y contratista general que trabaja en Austin, Texas, la ciudad donde nació y creció. Su estudio se centra en proyectos de construcción residencial, pequeños comercios y arte público. El enfoque de diseño de Nicole se basa en el cliente y el contexto, buscando soluciones novedosas que se adapten estrechamente a las necesidades y al estilo personal de sus clientes. En 2019, Elle Decor nombró a Nicole una de las mayores arquitectas vivas del mundo, junto con varios ganadores del Premio Pritzker. Sus proyectos han recibido numerosos premios de diseño, tanto locales como internacionales, y su trabajo ha sido publicado en libros, revistas y campañas publicitarias en todo el mundo. Obtuvo experiencia laboral temprana en las oficinas de Nueva York de los arquitectos Robert A.M. Stern y Peter Eisenman, y obtuvo una Licenciatura en Ciencias en Textiles y Confección de la Universidad de Cornell y una Maestría en Arquitectura de Rice.

Nicole Blair

www.nicoleblair.com

Nicole Blair

The Perch

Austin, Texas, USA // Photos © Casey Dunn

The Perch is a 61.32 m² studio shaped to fit above the existing bungalow roofline and just below the City of Austin setback tent limiting building height. Owners Annie and Dylan, a hairstylist and a landscape designer, wanted to keep their backyard intact, not move during construction, nor disrupt the mature landscape. The Perch rests on four steel columns, three of which pierce through existing bungalow walls to resist lateral forces. Shop-built steel framing was craned into place to minimally disturb the site. The cantilevered form gently sways in the wind, a reminder of its construction. Materials were selected for durability, economy, and serenity including whitewashed pine walls and ceilings (spanning from the exterior porch into the interior), maple butcher block countertops, and white oak flooring throughout.

The Perch ist ein 61,32 m² großes Studio, das so konzipiert wurde, dass es über der Dachlinie des vorhandenen Bungalows liegt und knapp unter der Höhenbegrenzung der Stadt Austin bleibt. Die Besitzer, Annie und Dylan, eine Stylistin und ein Landschaftsgestalter, wollten ihren Hinterhof intakt halten, während der Bau stattfand, und die Landschaft nicht stören. The Perch ruht auf vier Stahlsäulen, von denen drei die bestehenden Wände durchdringen, um seitliche Kräfte zu widerstehen. Der im Werk gebaute Stahlrahmen wurde mit einem Kran minimalinvasiv am Ort platziert. Die auskragende Form schaukelt sanft im Wind und erinnert an ihre Konstruktion. Die Materialien wurden aufgrund ihrer Haltbarkeit und Wirtschaftlichkeit ausgewählt, einschließlich gekalkter Kiefernwände und Decken (die vom äußeren Vordach bis ins Innere reichen), Ahornblock-Arbeitsplatten und weiße Eicheböden im gesamten Raum.

The Perch est un studio de 61,32 m² conçu pour s'adapter au-dessus de la ligne de toit du bungalow existant et juste en dessous de la limite de hauteur de construction de la ville d'Austin. Les propriétaires, Annie et Dylan, une styliste et un paysagiste, voulaient préserver leur arrière-cour, ne pas déménager pendant la construction et ne pas perturber le paysage. The Perch repose sur quatre colonnes en acier, dont trois traversent les murs existants pour résister aux forces latérales. Le cadre en acier construit en atelier a été placé avec une grue pour perturber le moins possible l'endroit. La forme en porte-à-faux se balance doucement dans le vent, rappelant sa construction. Les matériaux ont été sélectionnés pour leur durabilité et leur économie, notamment des murs et des plafonds en pin blanchi (s'étendant de la véranda extérieure à l'intérieur), des plans de travail en blocs d'érable et des sols en chêne blanc dans tout l'espace.

The Porch es un estudio de 61,32 m² diseñado para adaptarse por encima de la línea del techo del bungalow existente y justo debajo de la línea de la Ciudad de Austin que limita la altura de construcción. Los propietarios, Annie y Dylan, una estilista y un paisajista, querían mantener intacto su patio trasero, no mudarse durante la construcción ni perturbar el paisaje. The Perch descansa sobre cuatro columnas de acero, tres de las cuales atraviesan las paredes existentes para resistir las fuerzas laterales. El armazón de acero construido en taller se colocó con grúa para perturbar mínimamente el lugar. La forma en voladizo se balancea suavemente en el viento, recordando su construcción. Los materiales fueron seleccionados por su durabilidad y economía, incluyendo paredes y techos de pino encalado (que se extienden desde el porche exterior hasta el interior), encimeras de bloques de arce y pisos de roble blanco en todo el espacio.

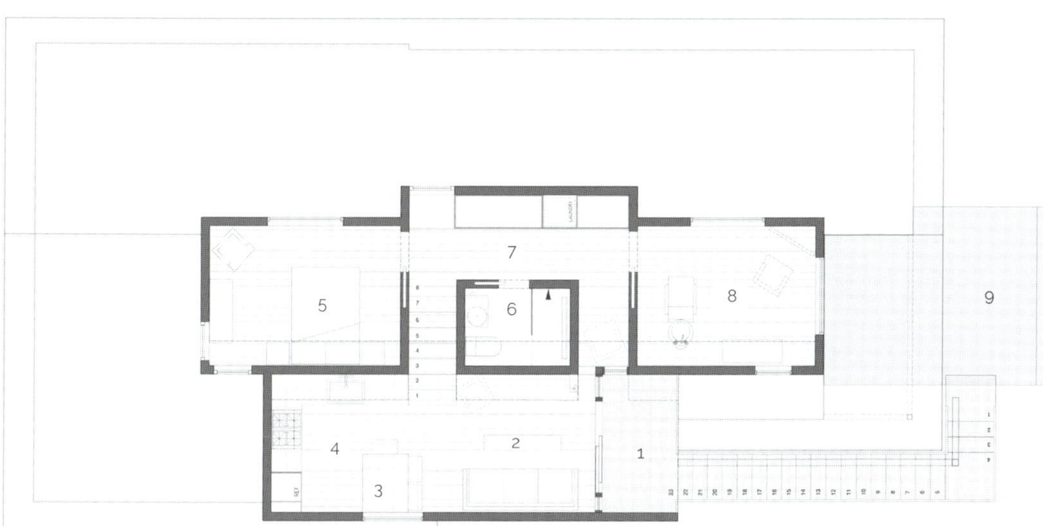

Floor plan

1. New covered porch
2. Living / Reception
3. Dining
4. Kitchen
5. Bedroom / Office 1
6. Bath
7. Hall
8. Bedroom / Office 2
9. Existing shared porch

Oslotre has been working uniquely with timber architecture and modern timber constructions for more than a decade, serving as an active and innovative driver for transformation in the building industry. Oslotre is a vision-driven office with an interdisciplinary team of architects, engineers, and carpenters who possess one of Europe's foremost expertise in timber architecture. With this unique team, Oslotre can offer a broad portfolio of innovative, biologically based buildings grounded in distinct architectural expertise in timber construction. Oslotre's goal is to contribute to a reduction in greenhouse gas emissions while enhancing the quality of our built environment and spaces. The transition towards a biological architecture will facilitate a societal shift from the past centuries' use-and-throw-away model to circular value chains in the building and real estate industry.

Oslotre arbeitet seit mehr als einem Jahrzehnt auf einzigartige Weise mit Holzarchitektur und modernen Holzkonstruktionen und ist ein aktiver und innovativer Motor für den Wandel in der Baubranche. Oslotre ist ein visionäres Büro mit einem interdisziplinären Team aus Architekten, Ingenieuren und Zimmerleuten, das in Europa über eines der größten Fachwissen in der Holzarchitektur verfügt. Mit diesem einzigartigen Team kann Oslotre ein breites Portfolio an innovativen, biologisch basierten Gebäuden anbieten, die auf einer ausgeprägten architektonischen Expertise im Holzbau basieren. Das Ziel von Oslotre ist es, zur Reduzierung der Treibhausgasemissionen beizutragen und gleichzeitig die Qualität unserer gebauten Umwelt und unserer Räume zu verbessern. Der Übergang zu einer biologischen Architektur wird einen gesellschaftlichen Wandel von dem jahrhundertealten Modell des Nutzens und Wegwerfens hin zu zirkulären Wertschöpfungsketten in der Bau- und Immobilienbranche ermöglichen..

Oslotre travaille de manière unique dans l'architecture en bois et les constructions modernes en bois depuis plus d'une décennie, en tant que moteur actif et innovant de la transformation de l'industrie du bâtiment. Oslotre est un bureau axé sur la vision avec une équipe interdisciplinaire d'architectes, d'ingénieurs et de charpentiers possédant l'une des expertises les plus importantes d'Europe en architecture en bois. Avec cette équipe unique, Oslotre peut proposer un large portefeuille de bâtiments innovants et biologiquement basés, ancrés dans une expertise architecturale distincte en construction bois. L'objectif d'Oslotre est de contribuer à une réduction des émissions de gaz à effet de serre tout en améliorant la qualité de notre environnement construit et de nos espaces. La transition vers une architecture biologique facilitera un changement sociétal du modèle de consommation et de jeté du passé vers des chaînes de valeur circulaires dans l'industrie du bâtiment et de l'immobilier.

Oslotre lleva más de una década trabajando de forma única con la arquitectura de madera y las construcciones modernas de madera, actuando como motor activo e innovador de la transformación en el sector de la construcción. Oslotre es una oficina visionaria que cuenta con un equipo interdisciplinar de arquitectos, ingenieros y carpinteros que poseen una de las mayores competencias de Europa en arquitectura de madera. Con este equipo único, Oslotre puede ofrecer una amplia cartera de edificios innovadores de base biológica basados en una experiencia arquitectónica distintiva en la construcción en madera. El objetivo de Oslotre es contribuir a la reducción de las emisiones de gases de efecto invernadero, mejorando al mismo tiempo la calidad de nuestro entorno y espacios construidos. La transición hacia una arquitectura biológica facilitará un cambio social desde el modelo de usar y tirar de los siglos pasados hacia cadenas de valor circulares en la industria de la construcción y el sector inmobiliario.

Oslotre

www.oslotre.no

Oslotre Team

V and L Cabin

Y Cabin

Norefjell, Norway // Photos © Kyrre Sundal

The V and L cabins, designed for two pairs of friends, perch atop a hillside overlooking Lake Krøderen in Norefjell, Norway. True to their names, the cabins consist of two adjacent volumes: one housing the bedrooms and the other featuring an open living and dining area. Notably, the living room is situated a few steps lower than the kitchen, creating a natural division between the spaces. Expansive windows in the living room face eastward, framing the captivating view of the valley below. In the evenings, the two fireplaces take center stage as the main focal points. Both cabins are constructed using solid masstimber, with wooden elements showcased prominently in the interior. The lightly treated walls and ceilings contribute to a breathable and healthy environment. On the exterior, ore pine cladding characterizes the cabins, complemented by contrasting accents in shades of dark red and dark green.

Die für zwei befreundete Paare konzipierten Hütten V und L liegen auf einem Hügel mit Blick auf den See Krøderen in Norefjell, Norwegen. Wie ihr Name schon sagt, bestehen die Hütten aus zwei nebeneinander liegenden Volumen: in einem befinden sich die Schlafzimmer, im anderen ein offener Wohn- und Essbereich. Das Wohnzimmer liegt ein paar Stufen tiefer als die Küche und schafft so eine natürliche Trennung zwischen den beiden Räumen. Die großen Fenster des Wohnzimmers sind nach Osten ausgerichtet und geben den Blick auf das darunter liegende Tal frei. In den Abendstunden sind die beiden Kamine der Mittelpunkt des Geschehens. Beide Hütten sind aus massivem Massivholz gebaut, wobei die Holzelemente im Innenraum besonders hervorgehoben werden. Die leicht behandelten Wände und Decken tragen zu einer atmungsaktiven und gesunden Umgebung bei. Außen sind die Hütten mit Erzkiefer verkleidet, die durch kontrastierende Akzente in Dunkelrot und Dunkelgrün ergänzt wird.

Les cabanes V et L, conçues pour deux couples d'amis, perchent au sommet d'une colline surplombant le lac Krøderen à Norefjell, en Norvège. Fidèles à leurs noms, les cabanes se composent de deux volumes adjacents : l'un abritant les chambres et l'autre proposant un espace de vie et de salle à manger ouvert. Notamment, le salon est situé quelques marches plus bas que la cuisine, créant une division naturelle entre les espaces. Les grandes fenêtres du salon donnent à l'est, encadrant la vue captivante sur la vallée en dessous. Le soir, les deux cheminées deviennent les points focaux principaux. Les deux cabanes sont construites en bois massif, avec des éléments en bois mis en valeur dans l'intérieur. Les murs et plafonds légèrement traités contribuent à un environnement respirant et sain. À l'extérieur, le revêtement en pin ore caractérise les cabanes, complété par des accents contrastés dans des teintes de rouge foncé et de vert foncé.

Las cabañas V y L, diseñadas para dos parejas de amigos, están situadas en lo alto de una colina con vistas al lago Krøderen, en Norefjell (Noruega). Fieles a su nombre, las cabañas constan de dos volúmenes adyacentes: uno alberga los dormitorios y el otro presenta una zona de estar y comedor abierta. El salón está situado unos escalones más abajo que la cocina, lo que crea una división natural entre los espacios. Los amplios ventanales del salón miran hacia el este, enmarcando la cautivadora vista del valle. Por la noche, las dos chimeneas se convierten en el centro de atención. Ambas cabañas están construidas con madera maciza, y los elementos de madera ocupan un lugar destacado en el interior. Las paredes y los techos ligeramente tratados contribuyen a crear un ambiente saludable. En el exterior, el revestimiento de pino mineral caracteriza las cabañas, complementado por acentos de contraste en tonos rojo y verde oscuro.

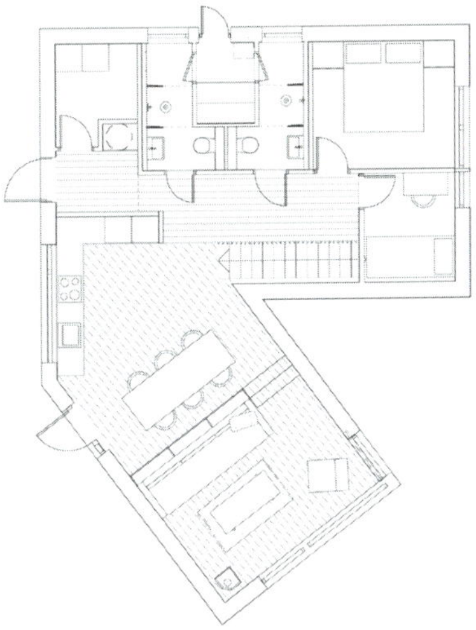

Floor plan of Cabin V

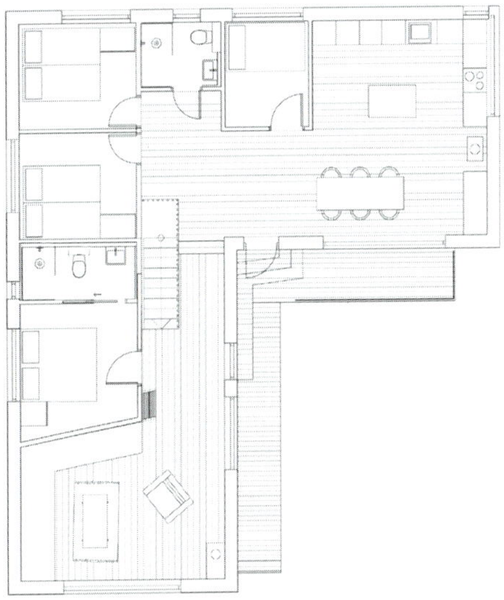

Floor plan of Cabin L

Ringerike, Norway // Photos © Kyrre Sundal, Nadia Norskott

The Y cabin is nestled in the Vikerfjell mountain range in Norway. The building volume branches out in three directions from a central pivot point, where six differently angled masstimber roof slabs meet and holds the building together. The floor plan is divided into three arms, one of which contains the bedrooms, while the two remaining arms are dedicated to the dining room and a living room/kitchen area that extends out to capture the breathtaking views of the mountain scapes. The fireplace, positioned at the center where the Y splits, not only provides warmth to both living spaces but also serves as the main focal point inside the cabin. The interior is characterized by visible CLT (cross-laminated timber) elements and ocher-colored Valchromat panels. The consistent use of solid wood throughout the building creates a warm and cozy indoor environment. The exterior is clad with ore pine, seamlessly blending the cabin into the surrounding forest landscape.

Die Y-Hütte liegt eingebettet in der Bergkette Vikerfjell in Norwegen. Das Gebäudevolumen verzweigt sich in drei Richtungen von einem zentralen Drehpunkt aus, an dem sechs unterschiedlich abgewinkelte Dachplatten aus Massivholz aufeinandertreffen und das Gebäude zusammenhalten. Der Grundriss ist in drei Arme unterteilt, von denen einer die Schlafzimmer beherbergt, während die beiden anderen Arme dem Esszimmer und einem Wohn-/Küchenbereich gewidmet sind, der sich nach außen erstreckt, um die atemberaubende Aussicht einzufangen. Der Kamin, der sich in der Mitte befindet, wo sich das Y teilt, spendet nicht nur Wärme für beide Wohnräume, sondern dient auch als zentraler Blickpunkt im Inneren der Hütte. Der Innenraum ist geprägt von sichtbaren CLT-Elementen (Brettsperrholz) und ockerfarbenen Valchromat-Paneelen. Das Äußere ist mit Erzkiefer verkleidet, wodurch sich die Hütte nahtlos in die umliegende Waldlandschaft einfügt.

La cabane Y est nichée dans la chaîne de montagnes Vikerfjell en Norvège. Le volume du bâtiment se divise en trois directions à partir d'un point de pivot central, où six dalles de toit en bois massif de différentes formes se rejoignent et maintiennent le bâtiment ensemble. Le plan d'étage est divisé en trois bras, l'un contenant les chambres à coucher, tandis que les deux bras restants sont dédiés à la salle à manger et à un salon/cuisine qui s'étend pour capturer les vues spectaculaires des paysages montagneux. La cheminée, positionnée au centre où la Y se divise, fournit non seulement de la chaleur aux deux espaces de vie, mais sert également de point focal principal à l'intérieur de la cabane. L'intérieur est caractérisé par des éléments visibles en CLT (bois lamellé croisé) et des panneaux de Valchromat de couleur ocre. L'utilisation cohérente du bois massif dans tout le bâtiment crée un environnement intérieur chaleureux et confortable. L'extérieur est habillé de pin ore, intégrant parfaitement la cabane dans le paysage forestier environnant.

La cabaña Y está enclavada on la cordillera de Vikerfjell, en Noruega. El volumen del edificio se ramifica en tres direcciones a partir de un punto de giro central, donde se juntan seis losas de techo de madera maciza con ángulos diferentes que mantienen unido el edificio. La planta se divide en tres brazos, uno de los cuales alberga los dormitorios, mientras que los dos restantes están dedicados al comedor y a una sala de estar/cocina que se extiende hacia fuera para captar las impresionantes vistas de los paisajes montañosos. La chimenea, situada en el centro donde se divide la Y, no sólo proporciona calor a ambos espacios vitales, sino que también sirve como punto focal principal dentro de la cabaña. El interior se caracteriza por elementos visibles de CLT (madera contralaminada) y paneles Valchromat de color ocre. El uso constante de madera maciza en todo el edificio crea un ambiente interior cálido y acogedor. El exterior está revestido de pino mineral, que integra perfectamente la cabaña en el paisaje forestal circundante.

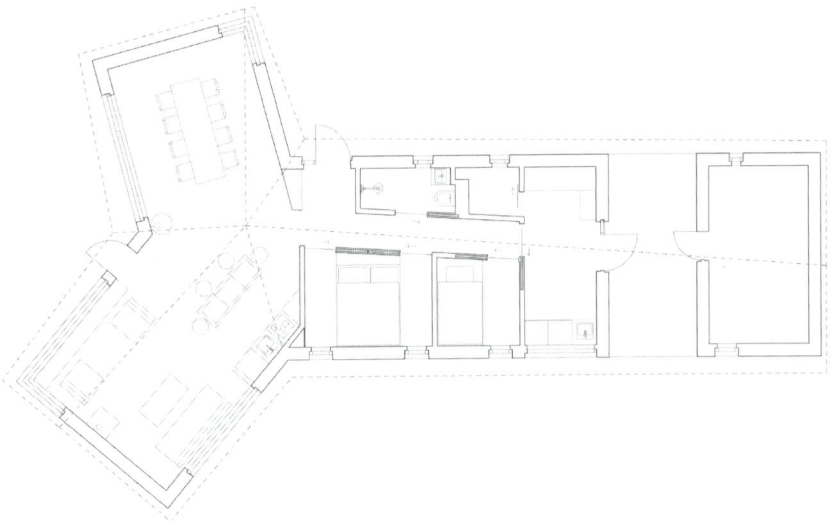

Floor plan

Paulo Martins Arquitectura assumes itself as a studio focused on experimental and strategic design, provoking and making the sensorial and emotional experiences part of the process and a goal to be achieved.
Through a holistic vision, we view and understand our work as a vehicle responsible for social, political, economical well-being and social equilibrium, assuming this responsibility as an opportunity to reinvent strategies and propose alternatives!
We project value-added buildings, designed to offer a high level of satisfaction and well-being, enhancing the relationship between dualities (interior / exterior, light / shade, soft / rough...), blurring their boundaries and diluting the barrier that separates them. We propose a sustainable and hedonistic architecture, free from preconception and stereotypes.

Paulo Martins Arquitectura versteht sich als ein Studio, das sich auf experimentelles und strategisches Design konzentriert, indem es sinnliche und emotionale Erfahrungen als Teil des Prozesses und des zu erreichenden Ziels provoziert und ermöglicht.
Mit einer ganzheitlichen Vision sehen und verstehen wir unsere Arbeit als verantwortungsbewusstes Mittel für soziales, politisches und wirtschaftliches Wohlergehen und soziales Gleichgewicht und nehmen diese Verantwortung als Chance wahr, Strategien neu zu erfinden und Alternativen vorzuschlagen.
Wir entwerfen Gebäude mit Mehrwert, die ein hohes Maß an Zufriedenheit und Wohlbefinden bieten, indem wir die Beziehung zwischen den Dualitäten (innen / außen, Licht / Schatten, weich / hart...) verbessern, ihre Grenzen verwischen und die Barriere, die sie trennt, aufweichen. Wir schlagen eine nachhaltige und hedonistische Architektur vor, die frei von Vorurteilen und Klischees ist.

Paulo Martins Arquitectura s'assume comme un studio axé sur la conception expérimentale et stratégique, provoquant et faisant des expériences sensorielles et émotionnelles une partie du processus et un objectif à atteindre.
Grâce à une vision holistique, nous voyons et comprenons notre travail comme un véhicule responsable du bien-être social, politique et économique et de l'équilibre social, assumant cette responsabilité comme une opportunité de réinventer des stratégies et de proposer des alternatives.
Nous concevons des bâtiments à valeur ajoutée, destinés à offrir un haut niveau de satisfaction et de bien-être, en valorisant la relation entre les dualités (intérieur / extérieur, lumière / ombre, doux / transparent...), en brouillant leurs limites et en diluant la barrière qui les sépare. Nous proposons une architecture durable et hédoniste, exempte d'idées préconçues et de stéréotypes.

Paulo Martins Arquitectura se asume como un estudio centrado en el diseño experimental y estratégico, provocando y haciendo de las experiencias sensoriales y emocionales parte del proceso y una meta a alcanzar.
A través de una visión holística, vemos y entendemos nuestro trabajo como un vehículo responsable del bienestar social, político, económico y del equilibrio social, asumiendo esta responsabilidad como una oportunidad para reinventar estrategias y proponer alternativas.
Proyectamos edificios de valor añadido, diseñados para ofrecer un alto nivel de satisfacción y bienestar, potenciando la relación entre dualidades (interior / exterior, luz / sombra, suave / rugoso...), difuminando sus límites y diluyendo la barrera que los separa. Proponemos una arquitectura sostenible y hedonista, libre de preconceptos y estereotipos.

Paulo Martins Arquitectura

www.paulomartins.com.pt

Paulo Martins

Park House

The Park House is located on a quiet, central street in the city of Aveiro, facing a natural, tree-filled area, the city park. It emerged from the alteration and expansion of a deteriorated Art Nouveau building constructed in the 20th century. The facade features various plant, animal, and human elements carved in limestone, whose architectural and historical value was essential to preserve. Respecting the memory inscribed in the building's original skin, the Park House unfolds towards the green heart of the city. Its stony body, extruded from the original facade and carved by wooden slats, cuts through space creating a visual narrative that celebrates the passage of time, with lines and shadows dancing to the rhythm of the years. Constructed with the soul of wood (CLT), the house is organized over four floors: a garage and workspace in the basement floor; the ground floor; the upper floors house four suites, and finally, a terrace that offers 360° views over the city.

Das Parkhaus befindet sich in einer ruhigen, zentralen Straße in Aveiro, mit Blick auf einen natürlichen, baumreichen Bereich, den Stadtpark. Es ist aus dem Umbau und der Erweiterung eines verfallenen Jugendstilgebäudes aus dem 20. Jahrhundert hervorgegangen. Die Fassade weist verschiedene in Kalkstein gehauene Elemente auf, deren architektonischer Wert unbedingt erhalten werden sollte. Sein steinerner Körper, der aus der ursprünglichen Fassade herausgearbeitet und mit Holzlatten versehen wurde, durchschneidet den Raum und schafft eine visuelle Erzählung, die den Lauf der Zeit feiert, mit Linien und Schatten, die im Rhythmus der Jahre tanzen. Das mit der Seele des Holzes (CLT) errichtete Haus erstreckt sich über vier Etagen: eine Garage und ein Arbeitsraum im Untergeschoss, das Erdgeschoss, die oberen Etagen mit vier Suiten und schließlich eine Terrasse, die einen 360°-Blick über die Stadt bietet.

La Maison do Parc est située dans une rue calme et centrale de la ville d'Aveiro, face à une zone naturelle arborée, le parc de la ville. Elle a émergé de la modification et de l'agrandissement d'un bâtiment Art Nouveau dégradé construit au XXe siècle. La façade présente divers éléments végétaux, animaux et humains sculptés dans la pierre calcaire, dont la valeur architecturale et historique était essentielle à préserver. Respectant la mémoire inscrite dans la peau originale du bâtiment, la Maison de Parc s'étend vers le cœur vert de la ville. Son corps en pierre, extrudé de la façade d'origine et sculpté de lattes de bois, découpe l'espace en créant une narration visuelle qui célèbre le passage du temps, avec des lignes et des ombres dansant au rythme des années. Construite avec l'âme du bois (CLT), la maison est organisée sur quatre étages : un garage et un espace de travail au sous-sol ; le rez-de-chaussée ; les étages supérieurs abritent quatre suites, et enfin, une terrasse offrant une vue à 360° sur la ville.

La Casa del Parque está situada en una tranquila y céntrica calle de la ciudad de Aveiro, frente a una zona natural y arbolada, el parque de la ciudad. Surgió de la reforma y ampliación de un edificio Art Nouveau deteriorado, construido en el siglo XX. La fachada presenta diversos elementos vegetales, animales y humanos tallados en piedra caliza, cuyo valor arquitectónico e histórico era esencial preservar. Respetando la memoria inscrita en la piel original del edificio, la Casa del Parque se despliega hacia el corazón verde de la ciudad. Su cuerpo pétreo, extruido de la fachada original y tallado por lamas de madera, recorta el espacio creando una narrativa visual que celebra el paso del tiempo, con líneas y sombras que bailan al ritmo de los años. Construida con el alma de la madera (CLT), la casa se organiza en cuatro plantas: un garaje y espacio de trabajo en la planta sótano, la planta baja, las plantas superiores que albergan cuatro suites y, por último, una terraza que ofrece vistas de 360° sobre la ciudad.

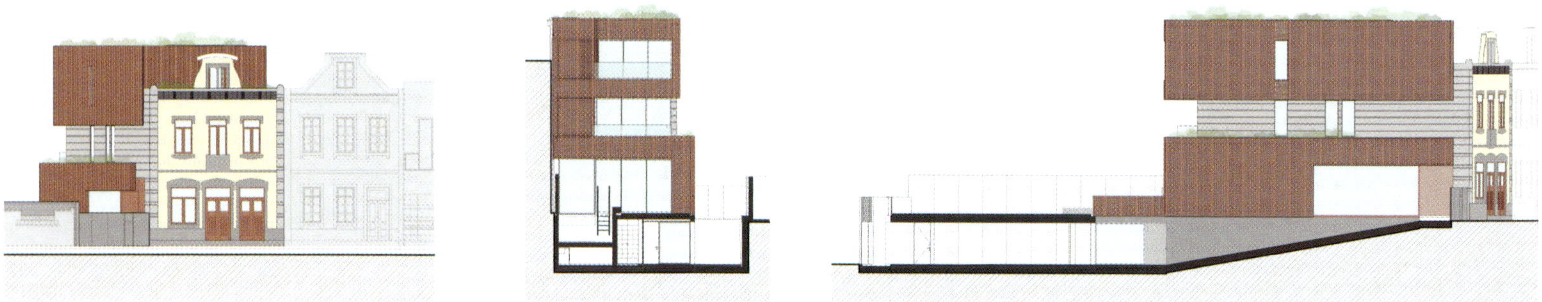

Elevations

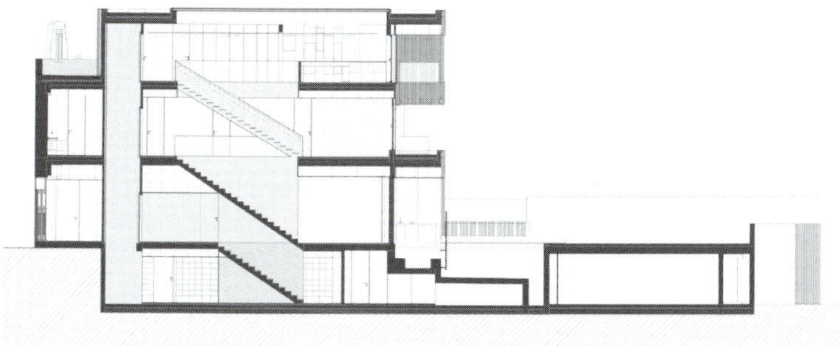

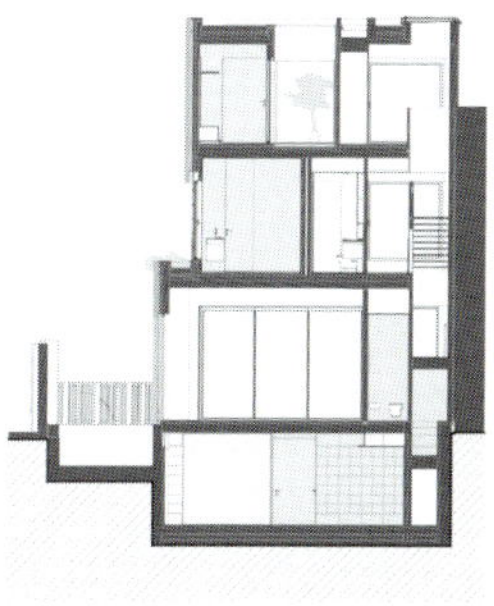

Sections

After spending many years working in both the architecture and construction industries, Peter Braithwaite established Peter Braithwaite Studio Ltd. in 2014 out of a desire to create a company that encompassed both design and construction. Since its establishment the company has completed many interesting residential and commercial projects, and has excelled in cabinetry and furniture design. Our dedication to design excellence, and the highest standards of craftsmanship, is evident in the execution of all our projects to date.

Our practice is located in Halifax, Nova Scotia, where proposed projects tend to lack large budgets or extraordinary resources. As a result our team must design and craft our work while pursuing unique and novel ways to add quality or 'value' without the requirement for expensive materials or complicated, time consuming, assemblies. Peter Braithwaite Studio represents the collaboration of a number of ambitious and dedicated individuals that share the common interest of exploring and implementing the benefits found in the intersection of design and construction.

Nachdem er viele Jahre sowohl in der Architektur- als auch in der Baubranche gearbeitet hatte, gründete Peter Braithwaite 2014 das Peter Braithwaite Studio Ltd. aus dem Wunsch heraus, ein Unternehmen zu gründen, das sowohl Design als auch Bau umfasst. Seit seiner Gründung hat das Unternehmen viele interessante Wohn- und Gewerbeprojekte abgeschlossen und sich im Bereich des Möbel- und Einrichtungsdesigns hervorgetan. Unser Engagement für exzellentes Design und höchste handwerkliche Standards zeigt sich in der Ausführung aller unserer bisherigen Projekte. Unser Büro befindet sich in Halifax, Nova Scotia, wo die vorgeschlagenen Projekte in der Regel nicht über große Budgets oder außergewöhnliche Ressourcen verfügen. Daher muss unser Team bei der Planung und Ausführung unserer Arbeiten einzigartige und neuartige Wege beschreiten, um die Qualität oder den „Wert" zu steigern, ohne dass teure Materialien oder komplizierte, zeitaufwändige Montagen erforderlich sind. Das Peter Braithwaite Studio ist das Ergebnis der Zusammenarbeit einer Reihe von ehrgeizigen und engagierten Personen, die das gemeinsame Interesse haben, die Vorteile zu erforschen und umzusetzen, die sich an der Schnittstelle von Design und Konstruktion ergeben.

Après avoir passé de nombreuses années à travailler dans les industries de l'architecture et de la construction, Peter Braithwaite a fondé Peter Braithwaite Studio Ltd. en 2014 dans le but de créer une entreprise englobant à la fois la conception et la construction. Depuis sa création, l'entreprise a réalisé de nombreux projets résidentiels et commerciaux intéressants, et s'est illustrée dans la conception de meubles et d'armoires. Notre dévouement à l'excellence en matière de conception et aux normes les plus élevées de l'artisanat est évident dans l'exécution de tous nos projets à ce jour. Notre pratique est située à Halifax, en Nouvelle-Écosse, où les projets proposés ont tendance à manquer de grands budgets ou de ressources extraordinaires. En conséquence, notre équipe doit concevoir et fabriquer notre travail tout en recherchant des moyens uniques et novateurs d'ajouter de la qualité ou de la « valeur » sans nécessiter de matériaux coûteux ou d'assemblages compliqués et longs. Peter Braithwaite Studio représente la collaboration de plusieurs individus ambitieux et dévoués partageant un intérêt commun pour l'exploration et la mise en œuvre des avantages trouvés dans l'intersection de la conception et de la construction.

Tras pasar muchos años trabajando en el sector de la arquitectura y en la construcción, Peter fundó Peter Braithwaite Studio Ltd. en 2014 por el deseo de crear una empresa que abarcara tanto el diseño como la construcción. Desde su creación, la empresa ha completado numerosos e interesantes proyectos residenciales y comerciales, y ha destacado en el diseño de ebanistería y mobiliario. La excelencia en el diseño y los más altos estándares de artesanía son evidentes en la ejecución de todos los proyectos hasta la fecha.

Nuestro despacho se encuentra en Halifax, Nueva Escocia, donde los proyectos propuestos suelen carecer de grandes presupuestos o recursos extraordinarios. Como resultado, nuestro equipo debe diseñar y elaborar nuestro trabajo buscando formas únicas y novedosas de añadir calidad o «valor» sin necesidad de materiales caros o montajes complicados y lentos. Peter Braithwaite Studio representa la colaboración de una serie de personas ambiciosas y dedicadas que comparten el interés común de explorar y poner en práctica los beneficios que se encuentran en la intersección del diseño y la construcción.

Peter Braithwaite Studio

www.peterbraithwaitestudio.com

Peter Braithwaite

Lambkill Ridge

The Sandbox

Terence Bay, Nova Scotia, Canada // Photos © Peter Braithwaite

Affectionately named, Lambkill Ridge has its moniker derived from the common name for a local plant, Sheep Laurel, which can be found in abundance along the barren lands of Terence Bay, Nova Scotia.
Designed as a getaway for a nature enthusiast young family of four, the architecture features two nearly identical volumes mirrored along a long, narrow boardwalk that connects the access road to the winding nature trails beyond. Hoisted up off the forest floor and trust into the tree canopy, the intention was to situate the user prominently into the natural environment, provide breathtaking views over the barren lands and out to the ocean from the loft spaces within, and encourage the natural landscape to continue to thrive throughout.
The long ascent up the two-tiered stairwell and along the boardwalk, provides views to the entrance of a subtle trailhead that is framed by the two darkened volumes.

Der liebevolle Name Lambkill Ridge leitet sich von der lokalen Pflanze Sheep Laurel ab, die in den kargen Böden der Terence Bay in Nova Scotia in großer Zahl vorkommt.
Das Haus wurde als Zufluchtsort für eine vierköpfige, naturbegeisterte Familie konzipiert und besteht aus zwei fast identischen Häusern, die sich entlang einer langen, schmalen Promenade spiegeln, die die Zufahrtsstraße mit den verschlungenen Naturpfaden dahinter verbindet. Durch den Aufstieg vom Waldboden und das Vertrauen in die Baumkronen sollte sich der Nutzer in die natürliche Umgebung einfügen, von den Lofträumen aus einen atemberaubenden Blick über das karge Land und auf den Ozean genießen und die natürliche Landschaft zum Gedeihen anregen.
Der lange Aufstieg über die zweistufige Treppe und entlang der Promenade gibt den Blick frei auf den Eingang zu einem subtilen Wanderweg, der von den beiden verdunkelten Volumen eingerahmt wird.

Affectueusement nommé, Lambkill Ridge tire son nom du nom commun d'une plante locale, le laurier des moutons, que l'on trouve en abondance le long des terres arides de Terence Bay, en Nouvelle-Écosse.
Conçue comme une escapade pour une jeune famille de quatre amateurs de nature, l'architecture présente deux volumes presque identiques, en miroir le long d'une longue passerelle étroite reliant la route d'accès aux sentiers naturels sinueux au-delà. Surélevée du sol forestier et poussée dans la canopée des arbres, l'intention était de situer l'utilisateur de manière proéminente dans l'environnement naturel, d'offrir des vues imprenables sur les terres arides et sur l'océan depuis les espaces en loft à l'intérieur, et d'encourager le paysage naturel à continuer de prospérer. La longue montée des deux escaliers à deux niveaux et le long de la passerelle offrent des vues sur l'entrée d'un sentier subtil encadré par les deux volumes assombris.

El cariñoso nombre de Lambkill Ridge procede del nombre común de una planta local, el «laurel de oveja», que abunda en las áridas tierras de Terence Bay, Nueva Escocia.
Diseñada como una escapada para una joven familia de cuatro miembros entusiasta de la naturaleza, la arquitectura presenta dos volúmenes casi idénticos que se reflejan a lo largo de un largo y estrecho paseo marítimo que conecta la carretera de acceso con los serpenteantes senderos naturales que hay más allá. Levantado del suelo del bosque y confiado en la copa de los árboles, la intención era situar al usuario en un lugar destacado del entorno natural, ofrecer unas vistas impresionantes de las tierras yermas y del océano desde los altillos interiores, y animar al paisaje natural a seguir prosperando.
El largo ascenso por la escalera de dos peldaños y a lo largo del paseo marítimo ofrece vistas a la entrada de un sutil sendero enmarcado por los dos volúmenes oscurecidos.

Bathurst, New Brunswick, Canada // Photos © Ema Peter

Inspired by the rugged beauty found in Bathurst, New Brunswick, architect Peter Braithwaite aspired to realize a dwelling that could withstand harsh coastal weather. During the initial site visit, the design team was confronted with horizontal rain and harsh winds that solidified the environmental factors that would drive the design process. The resulting home celebrates a connection to the natural environment and reinforces the importance of resilience. Named "The Sandbox", this cedar- clad home overlooks Chaleur Bay and offers expansive views down the beach and out to the open ocean. The design features generous windows and a rooftop patio accessed by an exterior, weathering steel staircase. Constructed with local building materials and techniques, The Sandbox stands as a testament to community collaboration and enduring craftsmanship, while offering its occupants a retreat that celebrates both the rugged beauty as well as the charm of New Brunswick.

Inspiriert von der rauen Schönheit von Bathurst, New Brunswick, wollte der Architekt Peter Braithwaite ein Haus bauen, das dem rauen Wetter an der Küste standhalten kann. Bei einem ersten Besuch vor Ort wurde das Planungsteam mit horizontalem Regen und heftigen Winden konfrontiert, was die Umweltfaktoren, die den Entwurfsprozess bestimmen sollten, verfestigte. Das entstandene Haus zelebriert die Verbindung zur natürlichen Umgebung und unterstreicht die Bedeutung der Widerstandsfähigkeit. Das mit Zedernholz verkleidete Haus mit dem Namen „The Sandbox" überblickt die Chaleur Bay und bietet einen weiten Blick auf den Strand und das offene Meer. Das Haus ist mit großzügigen Fenstern und einer Dachterrasse ausgestattet, die über eine Außentreppe aus verwittertem Stahl erreichbar ist. Gleichzeitig bietet es seinen Bewohnern einen Rückzugsort, der sowohl die raue Schönheit als auch den Charme von New Brunswick zelebriert.

Inspiré par la beauté sauvage de Bathurst, au Nouveau-Brunswick, l'architecte Peter Braithwaite a aspiré à réaliser une demeure capable de résister aux conditions météorologiques côtières difficiles. Lors de la visite initiale du site, l'équipe de conception a été confrontée à une pluie horizontale et à des vents violents qui ont solidifié les facteurs environnementaux qui allaient guider le processus de conception. La maison résultante célèbre une connexion avec l'environnement naturel et renforce l'importance de la résilience. Nommé « The Sandbox », cette maison revêtue de cèdre surplombe la baie des Chaleurs et offre une vue imprenable sur la plage et sur l'océan ouvert. Le design présente de généreuses fenêtres et un patio sur le toit accessible par un escalier extérieur en acier météorisé. The Sandbox est le témoignage d'une collaboration communautaire et d'un artisanat durable, tout en offrant à ses occupants un refuge qui célèbre à la fois la beauté sauvage et le charme du Nouveau-Brunswick.

Inspirado por la belleza agreste de Bathurst (Nuevo Brunswick), el arquitecto Peter Braithwaite aspiraba a realizar una vivienda que pudiera soportar las duras condiciones climáticas de la costa. Durante la visita inicial al emplazamiento, el equipo de diseño se enfrentó a lluvias horizontales y fuertes vientos que consolidaron los factores medioambientales que impulsarían el proceso de diseño. La casa resultante celebra la conexión con el entorno natural y refuerza la importancia de la resistencia. Bautizada como «The Sandbox», esta casa revestida de cedro se asoma a la bahía de Chaleur y ofrece amplias vistas de la playa y el océano abierto. El diseño presenta amplios ventanales y un patio en la azotea al que se accede por una escalera exterior de acero resistente a la intemperie. Construida con materiales y técnicas de construcción locales, The Sandbox es un testimonio de colaboración comunitaria y artesanía duradera, al tiempo que ofrece a sus ocupantes un refugio que celebra tanto la belleza agreste como el encanto de Nueva Brunswick.

GREAT
GOOD TO GREAT
DEAR EDWARD

GREAT
GOOD TO GREAT
DEAR EDWARD
HOWARD STERN COMES AGAIN
SOMEONE WE KNOW

Stanaćev Granados is a an architectural office founded by Nataša Stanaćev and Manu Granados, Serbian and Spanish architects respectively, with a base in Chile and Spain, and working internationally.
Our practice specializes in bespoke residential projects, characterized by a unique sensitivity toward the domestic life and material tactility. With each new project, we embrace a humble stance and allow our work to surge in a process where we genuinely listen to the clients' needs and meticulously explore the natural and material context of the project. Through innovative approaches and rigorous attention to detail, we strive to create singular and sustainable solutions that seamlessly blend into their surroundings, fostering exceptional everyday experiences.

Stanaćev Granados ist ein von Nataša Stanaćev und Manu Granados, einem serbischen bzw. spanischen Architekten, gegründetes Architekturbüro mit Sitz in Chile und Spanien, das international tätig ist.
Unser Büro hat sich auf maßgeschneiderte Wohnprojekte spezialisiert, die sich durch eine einzigartige Sensibilität für das häusliche Leben und die Taktilität der Materialien auszeichnen. Bei jedem neuen Projekt nehmen wir eine bescheidene Haltung ein und lassen unsere Arbeit in einem Prozess wachsen, in dem wir den Bedürfnissen der Kunden wirklich zuhören und den natürlichen und materiellen Kontext des Projekts sorgfältig erforschen. Durch innovative Ansätze und rigorose Liebe zum Detail streben wir danach, einzigartige und nachhaltige Lösungen zu schaffen, die sich nahtlos in ihre Umgebung einfügen und außergewöhnliche Alltagserlebnisse ermöglichen.

Stanaćev Granados est un bureau d'architecture fondé par Nataša Stanaćev et Manu Granados, architectes serbes et espagnols respectivement, avec une base au Chili et en Espagne, et travaillant à l'international.
Notre pratique est spécialisée dans les projets résidentiels sur mesure, caractérisés par une sensibilité unique envers la vie domestique et la tactilité des matériaux. Avec chaque nouveau projet, nous adoptons une approche humble et permettons à notre travail de surgir dans un processus où nous écoutons véritablement les besoins des clients et explorons méticuleusement le contexte naturel et matériel du projet. Grâce à des approches innovantes et une attention rigoureuse aux détails, nous nous efforçons de créer des solutions singulières et durables qui s'intègrent harmonieusement à leur environnement, favorisant des expériences quotidiennes exceptionnelles.

Stanaćev Granados es un estudio de arquitectura fundado por Nataša Stanaćev y Manu Granados, arquitectos serbio y español respectivamente, con sede en Chile y España, y que trabaja a nivel internacional.
Nuestro estudio se especializa en proyectos residenciales a medida, caracterizados por una sensibilidad única hacia la vida doméstica y la tactilidad de los materiales. Con cada nuevo proyecto, adoptamos una postura humilde y permitimos que nuestro trabajo surja en un proceso en el que escuchamos genuinamente las necesidades de los clientes y exploramos meticulosamente el contexto natural y material del proyecto. Mediante enfoques innovadores y una rigurosa atención al detalle, nos esforzamos por crear soluciones singulares y sostenibles que se integren perfectamente en su entorno, fomentando experiencias cotidianas excepcionales.

Stanaćev Granados

www.stanacev-granados.com

Nataša Stanaćev
Manu Granados

Casa Primeriza

Chorrillos, Chile // Photos © Marcos Zegers

Located on a small clearing within a cypress-filled hill sloping steeply toward the Pacific Ocean in Matanzas, Chile, Casa Primeriza was designed to encompass various moods and environments throughout the house. At the clients' request, it seamlessly integrates into the terrain, allowing occupants to utilize its multiple exterior spaces and make the most of outdoor living.
Anchored firmly atop its solid concrete base, the lighter and airier living spaces span two levels, with the main floor transitioning to the upper level through a double-height space. A cargo netting with an open weave divides this area, inviting children's play while facilitating uninterrupted family life between the two floors. Changes in the wood treatment, both in texture and color, enhance distinct atmospheres between the two floors.

Die Casa Primeriza befindet sich auf einer kleinen Lichtung inmitten eines mit Zypressen bewachsenen Hügels, der steil zum Pazifik in Matanzas, Chile, abfällt. Auf Wunsch der Bauherren fügt sich das Haus nahtlos in das Gelände ein und ermöglicht es den Bewohnern, die verschiedenen Außenbereiche zu nutzen und das Leben im Freien optimal zu gestalten. Auf dem soliden Betonsockel fest verankert, erstrecken sich die leichteren und luftigeren Wohnräume über zwei Ebenen, wobei das Hauptgeschoss durch einen doppelt so hohen Raum in das Obergeschoss übergeht. Ein Cargo-Netz mit offenem Geflecht teilt diesen Bereich und lädt die Kinder zum Spielen ein, während es gleichzeitig ein ungestörtes Familienleben zwischen den beiden Etagen ermöglicht. Veränderungen in der Holzbehandlung, sowohl in der Textur als auch in der Farbe, verstärken die unterschiedlichen Atmosphären zwischen den beiden Etagen.

Située sur une petite clairière au sein d'une colline remplie de cyprès descendant abruptement vers l'océan Pacifique à Matanzas, au Chili, Casa Primeriza a été conçue pour englober diverses humeurs et ambiances tout au long de la maison. À la demande des clients, elle s'intègre harmonieusement dans le terrain, permettant aux occupants d'utiliser ses multiples espaces extérieurs et de profiter au maximum de la vie en plein air. Ancrés fermement au sommet de leur base en béton solide, les espaces de vie plus légers et aérés s'étendent sur deux niveaux, le rez-de-chaussée se transformant en étage supérieur par le biais d'un espace à double hauteur. Un filet de chargement avec une maille ouverte divise cet espace, invitant au jeu des enfants tout en facilitant une vie familiale ininterrompue entre les deux étages. Des changements dans le traitement du bois, tant en texture qu'en couleur, renforcent les atmosphères distinctes entre les deux étages.

Situada en un pequeño claro dentro de una colina llena de cipreses con una pronunciada pendiente hacia el Océano Pacífico en Matanzas, Chile, Casa Primeriza fue diseñada para abarcar varios estados de ánimo y ambientes en toda la casa. A petición de los clientes, se integra perfectamente en el terreno, lo que permite a los ocupantes utilizar sus múltiples espacios exteriores y aprovechar al máximo la vida al aire libre.
Anclados firmemente sobre su sólida base de hormigón, los espacios habitables, más ligeros y ventilados, abarcan dos niveles, con la planta principal en transición al nivel superior a través de un espacio de doble altura. Una red de carga con trama abierta divide esta zona, invitando al juego de los niños y facilitando al mismo tiempo la vida familiar ininterrumpida entre las dos plantas. Los cambios en el tratamiento de la madera, tanto en textura como en color, realzan los distintos ambientes entre las dos plantas.

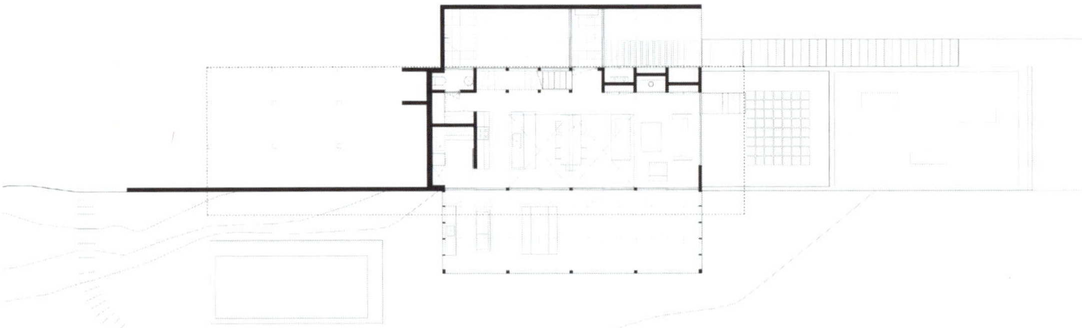

First floor plan

Surf Shacks

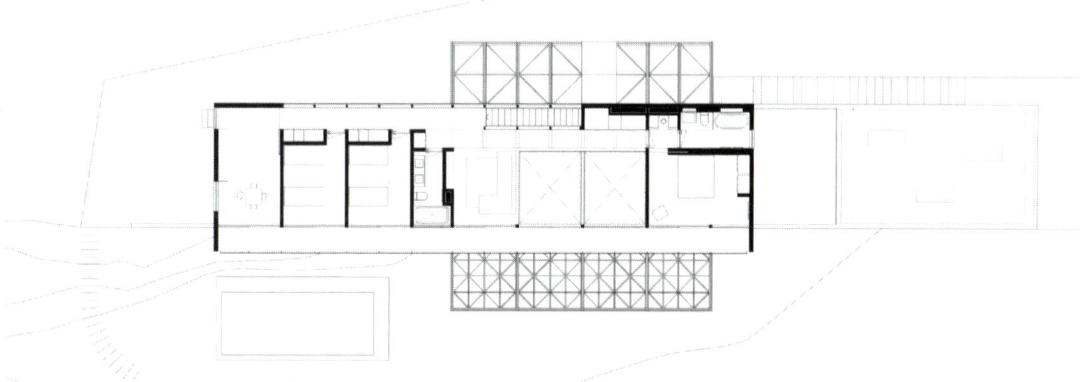

Second floor plan

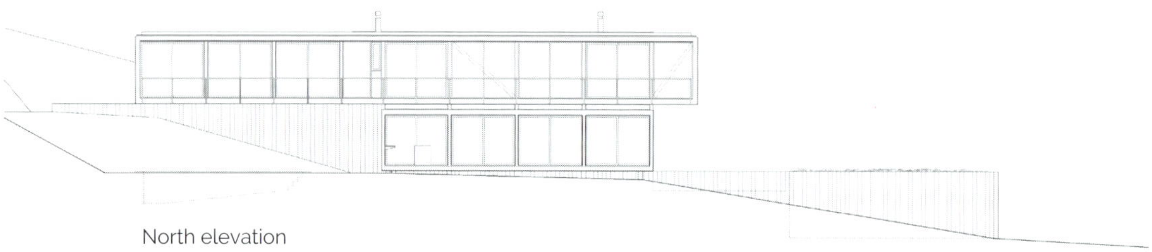

North elevation

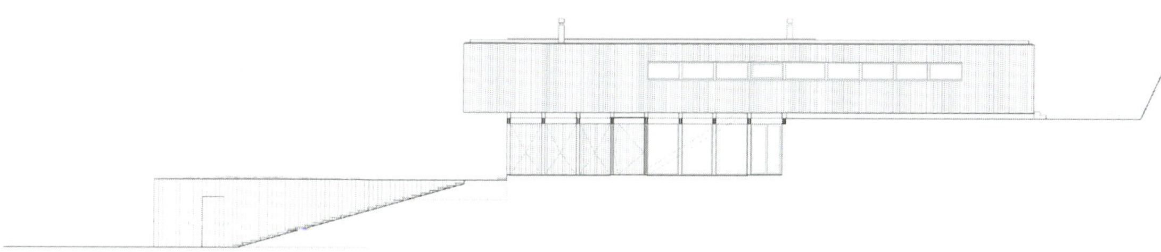

South elevation

The architecture of STUDIO AMB is based on each of the two founder's diverse expertise. After studying architecture in Tokyo and Paris, Haruki acquired a deep technical knowledge of architecture, construction and detail, as well as concept making at an organization design office (Tokyo) and an atelier design office (Paris).
Yosuke has worked across fields of art and product design (Tokyo), architecture (Paris), and interior design (Shanghai). Through such experience, he has cultivated a high sensitivity and multidisciplinary perspective. The overlapping of history, heritage and diverse cultural customs of multiple cities inspire the design vision of STUDIO AMB. This is then expressed through a fluid/equivocal interpretation that crosses scales and functions, from large-scale architecture to small products, and is created by mixing such different elements.

Die Architektur von STUDIO AMB basiert auf dem vielfältigen Wissen seiner beiden Gründer. Nach dem Architekturstudium in Tokio und Paris erwarb Haruki ein tiefes technisches Verständnis für Architektur, Bau und Detail, sowie für die Entwicklung von Konzepten in einem Designbüro (Tokio) und einem Atelier (Paris).
Yosuke arbeitete in den Bereichen Kunst und Produktdesign (Tokio), Architektur (Paris) und Innenarchitektur (Shanghai). Dank dieser Erfahrung hat er eine große Sensibilität und eine multidisziplinäre Perspektive entwickelt. Die Überlagerung von Geschichte, Erbe und verschiedenen kulturellen Bräuchen mehrerer Städte inspiriert die Designvision von STUDIO AMB. Dies wird durch eine fließende/uneindeutige Interpretation ausgedrückt, die Funktionen von groß angelegter Architektur bis hin zu kleinen Produkten durchmischt.

L'architecture du STUDIO AMB est basée sur les diverses connaissances de ses deux fondateurs. Après avoir étudié l'architecture à Tokyo et à Paris, Haruki a acquis une connaissance technique approfondie de l'architecture, de la construction et du détail, ainsi que de la création de concepts dans un bureau de conception d'organisations (Tokyo) et dans un atelier de conception (Paris).
Yosuke a travaillé dans les domaines de l'art et du design de produits (Tokyo), de l'architecture (Paris) et du design d'intérieur (Shanghai). Grâce à cette expérience, il a cultivé une grande sensibilité et une perspective multidisciplinaire. La superposition de l'histoire, du patrimoine et des diverses coutumes culturelles de plusieurs villes inspire la vision de conception du STUDIO AMB. Cela s'exprime à travers une interprétation fluide/équivoque qui traverse les fonctions, de l'architecture à grande échelle aux petits produits, en mélangeant des éléments si différents.

La arquitectura de STUDIO AMB se basa en los diversos conocimientos de sus dos fundadores. Tras estudiar arquitectura en Tokio y Paris, Haruki adquirió un profundo conocimiento técnico de la arquitectura, la construcción y el detalle, así como de la creación de conceptos en una oficina de diseño de organizaciones (Tokio) y en una oficina de diseño de atelier (Paris).
Yosuke ha trabajado en los campos del arte y el diseño de productos (Tokio), la arquitectura (Paris) y el diseño de interiores (Shanghai). Gracias a esta experiencia, ha cultivado una gran sensibilidad y una perspectiva multidisciplinar. La superposición de la historia, el patrimonio y las diversas costumbres culturales de múltiples ciudades inspiran la visión del diseño de STUDIO AMB. Esto se expresa a través de una interpretación fluida/equívoca que atraviesa funciones, desde la arquitectura a gran escala hasta los pequeños productos, mezclando elementos tan diferentes.

Studio AMB

www.s-amb.com

Haruki Nakayama
Yosuke Tsukamoto

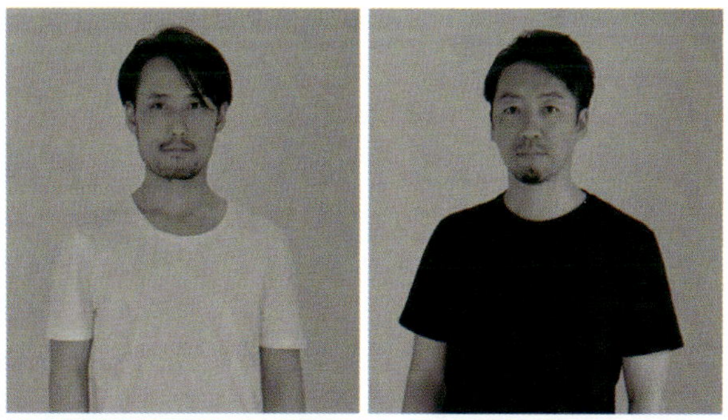

Misumi Annex

Shimane, Japan // Photos © Ryo Tsuchida

This project involves the renovation of a 120-year-old traditional wooden house in the Misumi region of Shimane (Japan) into an accommodation facility.
It is built directly on a stone foundation and is almost semi-outdoor, with only a wooden door as an external wall to blow the wind.
By reinterpreting the idea of the traditional Japanese earthen floor and placing the functions of daily life, such as cooking and bathing, in a space on the ground floor that was dug into the ground and made into a single unit, a new protected space was created that is continuous with the external space, but enclosed at shoulder height.
Through this open yet enclosed earthen floor space, it is intended to function as a place where people can directly feel the unique climate of the region and learn about the culture of gathering and interaction.

Dieses Projekt beinhaltet die Renovierung eines traditionellen 120 Jahre alten Holzhauses in der Region Misumi, Shimane (Japan), um es in eine Unterkunft umzuwandeln.
Es ist direkt auf einem Steinsockel gebaut und ist fast halb offen, mit nur einer hölzernen Tür als äußere Wand, um den Wind abzuhalten.
Durch die Neuinterpretation der Idee des traditionellen japanischen Erdgeschosses und die Anordnung der Funktionen des täglichen Lebens wie Kochen und Waschen in einem in den Boden gegrabenen und zu einer einzigen Einheit umgewandelten Raum wurde ein neuer geschützter Raum geschaffen, der mit der äußeren Umgebung verbunden ist, aber auf Schulterhöhe geschlossen ist.
Dieser offene, aber geschlossene Erdgeschossraum soll als Ort dienen, an dem die Menschen das einzigartige Klima der Region direkt spüren und etwas über die Kultur des Treffens und der Interaktion lernen können.

Ce projet consiste en la rénovation d'une maison traditionnelle en bois de 120 ans dans la région de Misumi, à Shimane (Japon), pour la transformer en logement. Elle est construite directement sur des fondations en pierre et est presque semi-extérieure, avec seulement une porte en bois comme mur extérieur pour supporter le vent. En réinterprétant l'idée du sol traditionnel en terre japonais et en plaçant les fonctions de la vie quotidienne, comme cuisiner et se laver, dans un espace du rez-de-chaussée creusé dans le sol et transformé en une seule unité, un nouvel espace protégé a été créé qui est continu avec l'espace extérieur, mais fermé à la hauteur des épaules.
Cet espace de sol en terre ouvert mais fermé est censé fonctionner comme un lieu où les gens peuvent ressentir directement le climat unique de la région et apprendre sur la culture de la rencontre et de l'interaction.

Este proyecto consiste en la renovación de una casa tradicional de madera de 120 años de antigüedad en la región de Misumi, en Shimane (Japón), para convertirla en un alojamiento.
Está construida directamente sobre unos cimientos de piedra y es casi semi exterior, con sólo una puerta de madera como muro exterior para que soporte el viento.
Al reinterpretar la idea del suelo de tierra tradicional japonés y situar las funciones de la vida cotidiana, como cocinar y asearse, en un espacio de la planta baja excavado en el suelo y convertido en una sola unidad, se creó un nuevo espacio protegido que es continuo con el espacio exterior, pero cerrado a la altura de los hombros. Este espacio de suelo de tierra abierto pero cerrado, se pretende que funcione como un lugar donde la gente pueda sentir directamente el clima único de la región y aprender sobre la cultura de la reunión y la interacción.

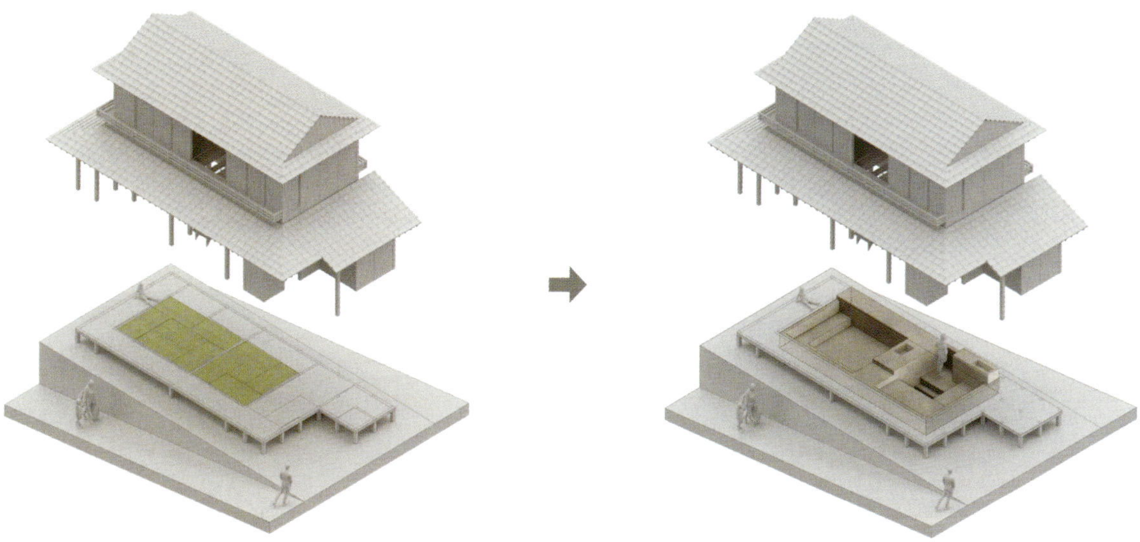

Axonometric view

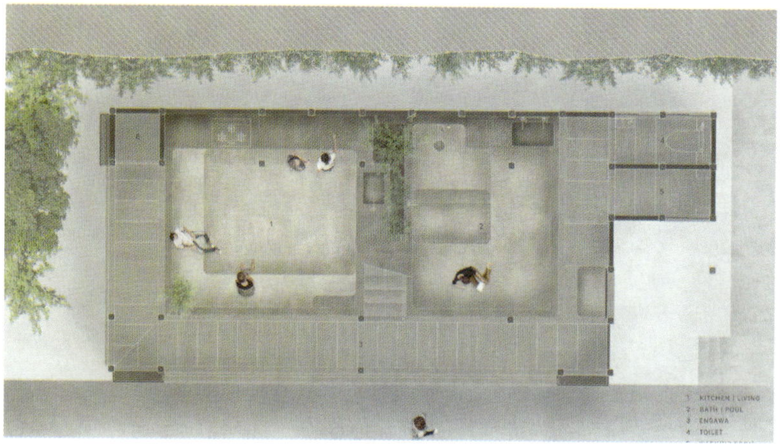

Ground floor plan

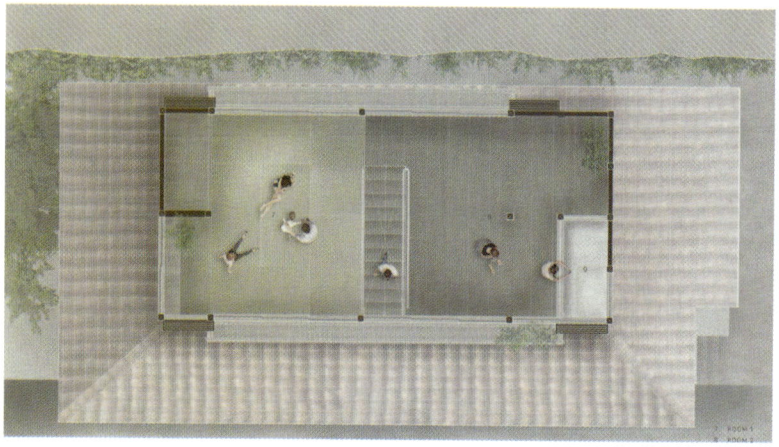

First floor plan

1. Kitchen / Living
2. Bath / Pool
3. Engawa
4. Toilet
5. Washing room
6. Storage
7. Room 1
8. Room 2
9. Void

Section

We are an architectural design and build studio specializing in ecological construction using durable, high quality and local materials, such as straw, wood and raw earth, applied with precision and care by our own construction company. We are based in Prague, the heart of Europe, and work internationally. Construction activities, primarily with clay, straw and wood, preceded our design work. The two buildings featured here showcase a creative development, from an initially less formally characterized design approach of The House of Violin Maker, which strives in an almost pre-architectural way for an organic fluidity of space, towards a more contextual and referential approach of Casa de mi Luna, which nevertheless retains some of the early ideas of organic fluidity. Both houses are built and designed by our respective studio and construction company. Intertwined and interdependent, the construction activities form an experiential base for design ideas to unfold and emerge, while the tapping into of the realm of design fuels the desire for unfettered creative activity to push the boundaries of ecological architecture.

Wir sind ein Architektur- und Bauunternehmen, das auf ökologisches Bauen mit langlebigen, hochwertigen und lokalen Materialien wie Stroh, Holz und Lehm spezialisiert ist, die präzise und sorgfältig von unserem eigenen Bauunternehmen angewendet werden. Unser Hauptsitz befindet sich in Prag, dem Herzen Europas, und wir arbeiten international. Der Bau, hauptsächlich mit Lehm, Stroh und Holz, ging unserem Designvorgang voraus. Die beiden hier vorgestellten Gebäude zeigen eine kreative Entwicklung von einem anfänglich weniger formal geprägten Designansatz wie bei der Haus eines Geigenbauers, die sich auf eine nahezu vor-architektonische Weise um eine organische Raumflüssigkeit bemüht, hin zu einem stärker kontextuellen und referenziellen Ansatz wie bei der Haus meines Mondes die jedoch einige der frühen Ideen zur organischen Flüssigkeit bewahrt. Beide Häuser wurden von unseren jeweiligen Design- und Bauunternehmen gebaut und entworfen. Verflochten und voneinander abhängig bilden die Bauaktivitäten eine experimentelle Basis, auf der Designideen entwickelt und hervorgebracht werden können, während das Design den Wunsch nach uneingeschränkter kreativer Aktivität zur Erweiterung der Grenzen der ökologischen Architektur nährt.

Nous sommes un studio de design architectural et de construction spécialisé dans la construction écologique avec des matériaux durables, de haute qualité et locaux, tels que la paille, le bois et la terre crue, appliqués avec précision et soin par notre propre entreprise de construction. Nous sommes basés à Prague, au cœur de l'Europe, et nous travaillons à l'échelle internationale. Les activités de construction, principalement avec de l'argile, de la paille et du bois, ont précédé notre travail de conception. Les deux bâtiments présentés ici montrent un développement créatif, passant d'une approche de conception initialement moins caractérisée formellement que La Maison du Luthier, qui s'efforce d'une manière presque pré-architecturale pour une fluidité organique de l'espace, vers une approche plus contextuelle et référentielle de la Maison de ma Lune, qui conserve cependant certaines des premières idées de fluidité organique. Les deux maisons ont été construites et conçues par nos propres studios et entreprises de construction respectifs. Intertwining et interdépendantes, les activités de construction forment une base expérimentale pour que les idées de conception se développent et émergent, tandis que l'exploitation de la conception nourrit le désir d'une activité créative sans restrictions pour repousser les limites de l'architecture écologique.

Somos un estudio de diseño arquitectónico y construcción especializado en la construcción ecológica con materiales duraderos, de alta calidad y locales, como paja, madera y tierra cruda, aplicados con precisión y cuidado por nuestra propia empresa constructora. Tenemos nuestra sede en Praga, el corazón de Europa, y trabajamos a escala internacional. Las actividades de construcción, principalmente con arcilla, paja y madera, precedieron a nuestro trabajo de diseño. Los dos edificios aquí presentados muestran un desarrollo creativo, desde un enfoque de diseño inicialmente menos caracterizado formalmente que La Casa del Fabricante de Violines, que se esfuerza de una manera casi pre-arquitectónica por una fluidez orgánica del espacio, hacia el enfoque más contextual y referencial de la Casa de mi Luna, que sin embargo conserva algunas de las primeras ideas de fluidez orgánica. Ambas casas han sido construidas y diseñadas por nuestros respectivos estudio y empresa constructora. Entrelazadas e interdependientes, las actividades de construcción forman una base experimental para que las ideas de diseño se desarrollen y surjan, mientras que el aprovechamiento del diseño alimenta el deseo de una actividad creativa sin restricciones para ampliar los límites de la arquitectura ecológica.

Studio Circle Growth & Terra Sylva Construction

www.studiocirclegrowth.com

Martin Žižka

Casa de mi Luna

House of a Violin Maker

The outer form and appearance needed to conform to local regulation as the house is on the edge of the Český kras nature reserve. Thus the house, built with straw Ecococon panels, aligns with the local vernacular; a simple symmetrical gable roof, rounded eaves, traditional rounded clay roof tiles called "bobrovka", and a mixed lime render and larch cladding facade.
The design of the interior is more open and playful than a typical Czech house. The almost completely open ground floor is determined by a segmented staircase which curves up into the double height space of the second floor landing. The staircase delineates the zones of the ground floor while simultaneously creating a gentle porosity between them. The two opposing, symmetrical rooms on the second floor feature an arched ceiling as a result of a creative collar tie solution for the rafters. The interiors are dominated by larch, pine and spruce in contrast to the soft white clay plaster, with terracotta tiles from a nearby village factory.

Die äußere Form und Erscheinung sollten den örtlichen Vorschriften entsprechen, da sich das Haus am Rand des Naturschutzgebiets von Český kras befindet. Das Haus, gebaut mit Ecococon-Strohplatten, passt zum örtlichen vernakulären Stil: ein einfaches, symmetrisches Satteldach, abgerundete Traufen, traditionelle Tonziegel namens „Bobrovka" und eine Mischfassade aus Kalkputz und Lärchenverkleidung. Das Innendesign ist offener und verspielter als das einer typischen tschechischen Haus. Das Erdgeschoss wird durch eine gestufte Treppe bestimmt, die sich zum doppelten Höhenraum der Lande des zweiten Stocks hinbiegt. Die Treppe grenzt die Bereiche des Erdgeschosses ab und schafft gleichzeitig eine sanfte Porosität zwischen ihnen. Die beiden gegenüberliegenden, symmetrischen Zimmer im zweiten Stock haben ein gewölbtes Dach, das das Ergebnis einer kreativen Balkenverbindungslösung ist. Die Innenräume werden von Lärche, Kiefer und Tanne dominiert und bilden einen Kontrast zu dem weichen, weißen Lehmputz mit Terrakottafliesen aus einer Fabrik in einem nahe gelegenen Dorf.

La forme et l'aspect extérieur devaient être conformes à la réglementation locale, car la maison est située en bordure de la réserve naturelle de Český kras. Ainsi, la maison, construite avec des panneaux de paille Ecococon, s'adapte au style vernaculaire local : un simple toit à deux versants symétrique, des avant-toits arrondis, des tuiles d'argile traditionnelles appelées « bobrovka », et une façade mixte de crépi à la chaux et de revêtement de mélèze. Le design intérieur est plus ouvert et ludique que celui d'une maison tchèque typique. Le rez-de-chaussée est déterminé par un escalier segmenté qui se courbe vers l'espace à double hauteur du palier du deuxième étage. L'escalier délimite les zones du rez-de-chaussée. Les deux chambres opposées et symétriques du deuxième étage présentent un plafond voûté, résultat d'une solution créative de liaison des poutres. Les intérieurs sont dominés par le mélèze, le pin et le sapin en contraste avec le plâtre doux en argile blanche, avec des carreaux de terre cuite provenant d'une usine d'un village voisin.

La forma y el aspecto exteriores debían ajustarse a la normativa local, ya que la casa se encuentra al borde de la reserva natural de Český kras. Así, la casa, construida con paneles de paja Ecococon, se ajusta al estilo vernáculo local: un sencillo tejado simétrico a dos aguas, aleros redondeados, tejas de arcilla tradicionales llamadas «bobrovka», y una fachada mixta de revoco de cal y revestimiento de alerce.
El diseño del interior es más abierto y lúdico que el de una típica casa checa. La planta baja está determinada por una escalera segmentada que se curva hacia el espacio de doble altura del rellano del segundo piso y delimita las zonas de la planta baja al tiempo que crea una suave porosidad entre ellas. Las dos habitaciones opuestas y simétricas de la segunda planta presentan un techo arqueado, resultado de una creativa solución de atado de las vigas. Los interiores están dominados por el alerce, el pino y el abeto en contraste con el suave enlucido de arcilla blanca, con baldosas de terracota procedentes de una fábrica de un pueblo cercano.

Site plan

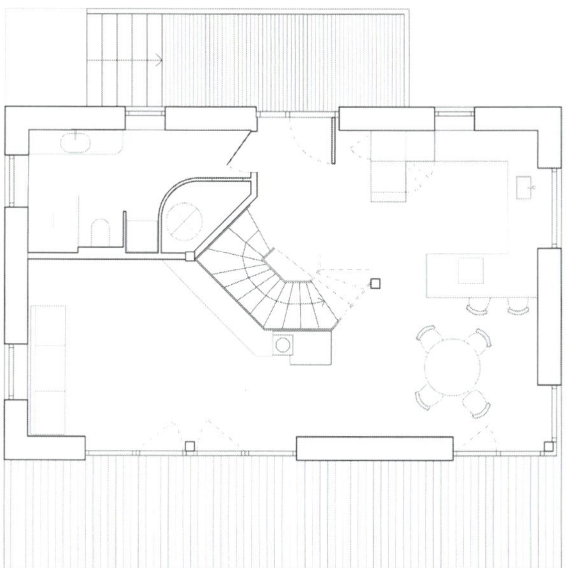

First floor plan

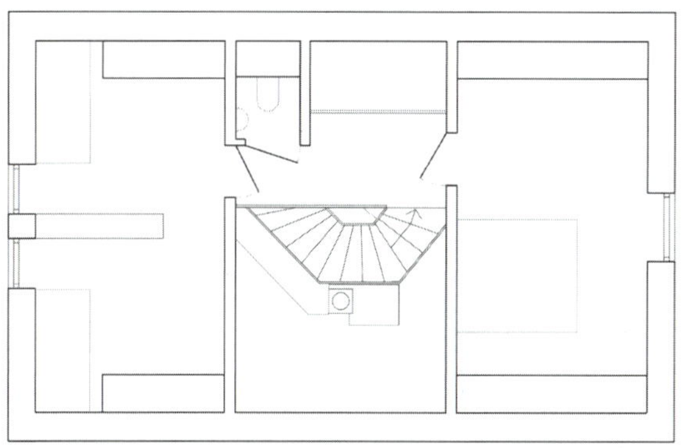

Second floor plan

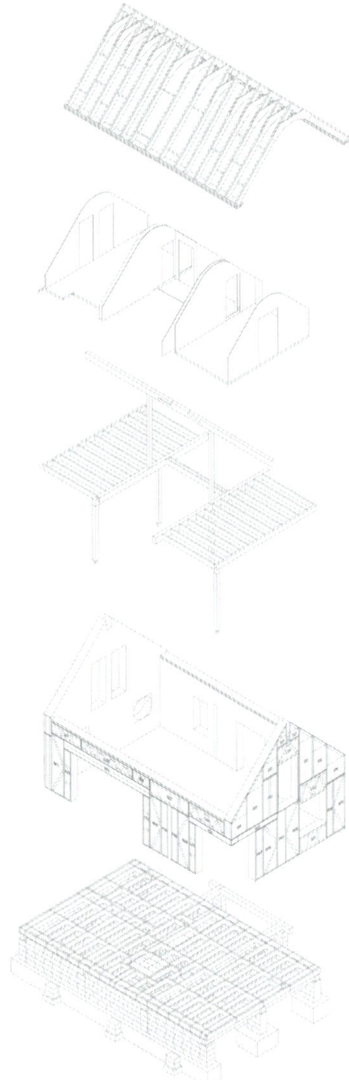

Axonometric details

The design of the house is based on an idea about a circular plan which spirals upward around a central dining table. The house is situated at the back of a narrow south-facing plot surrounded by birches, oaks and cedars, allowing continued use of the front portion of the plot for gardening and fruit trees. The idea that each space in the house would be gradually and incrementally higher than the preceding one was determined early on during the first conceptual drawings. The height of the living room, at two steps, is determined by the height of a terrace encircling the south part of the house. The height is also inspired by the elevation of Japanese houses and the tradition of always taking shoes off before entering an interior space. The first threshold is height. The house is built with timber and straw, and finished with a soft white clay plaster.

Das Design des Hauses basiert auf einer Idee eines kreisförmigen Grundrisses, der sich spiralförmig um einen zentralen Esstisch windet. Das Haus befindet sich auf der Rückseite eines schmalen Grundstücks, das nach Süden ausgerichtet ist und von Birken, Eichen und Zedern umgeben ist, was es ermöglicht, den vorderen Teil des Grundstücks weiterhin für Gartenarbeit und Obstbäume zu nutzen. Die Idee, dass jeder Raum des Hauses graduell und progressiv höher sein sollte als der vorherige, wurde bereits in den frühen konzeptionellen Zeichnungen festgelegt. Die Höhe des Wohnzimmers, um zwei Stufen erhöht, wird durch die Höhe einer Terrasse bestimmt, die den südlichen Teil des Hauses umgibt und von der Erhöhung der japanischen Häuser und der Tradition des immer vor dem Betreten eines Innenraums ausgezogenen Schuhwerks inspiriert ist. Die erste Schwelle ist die Höhe. Das Haus ist aus Holz und Stroh gebaut und mit einem weichen, weißen Lehmputz versehen.

Le design de la maison est basé sur l'idée d'un plan circulaire qui monte en spirale autour d'une table à manger centrale. La maison est située à l'arrière d'une parcelle étroite orientée au sud et entourée de bouleaux, de chênes et de cèdres, ce qui permet de continuer à utiliser la partie avant du terrain pour le jardinage et les arbres fruitiers. L'idée que chaque espace de la maison soit graduellement et progressivement plus haut que le précédent a été déterminée dès les premiers croquis conceptuels. La hauteur du salon, de deux marches, est déterminée par celle d'une terrasse qui entoure la partie sud de la maison et s'inspire de l'élévation des maisons japonaises et de la tradition de se déchausser toujours avant d'entrer dans un espace intérieur. Le premier seuil est la hauteur. La maison est construite en bois et en paille, et finie avec un plâtre doux en argile blanche.

El diseño de la casa se basa en una idea de planta circular que asciende en espiral en torno a una mesa de comedor central. La casa está situada en la parte trasera de una estrecha parcela orientada al sur y rodeada de abedules, robles y cedros, lo que permite seguir utilizando la parte delantera del terreno para la jardinería y los árboles frutales. La idea de que cada espacio de la casa fuera gradual y progresivamente más alto que el anterior se determinó ya en los primeros dibujos conceptuales. La altura del salón, de dos escalones, viene determinada por la de una terraza que rodea la parte sur de la casa y se inspira en la elevación de las casas japonesas y en la tradición de descalzarse siempre antes de entrar en un espacio interior. El primer umbral es la altura. La casa está construida con madera y paja, y acabada con un suave enlucido de arcilla blanca.

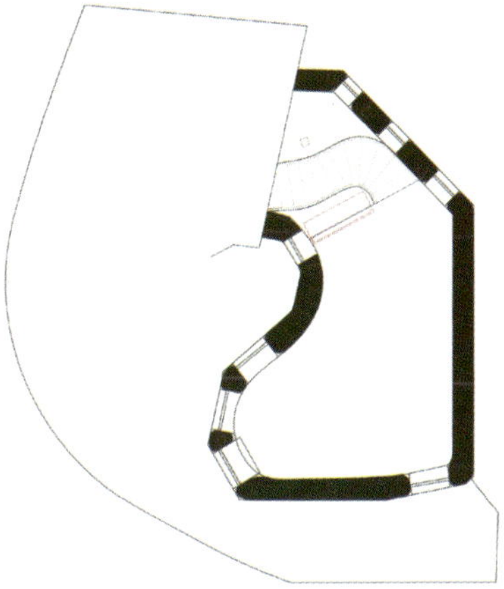

First floor plan

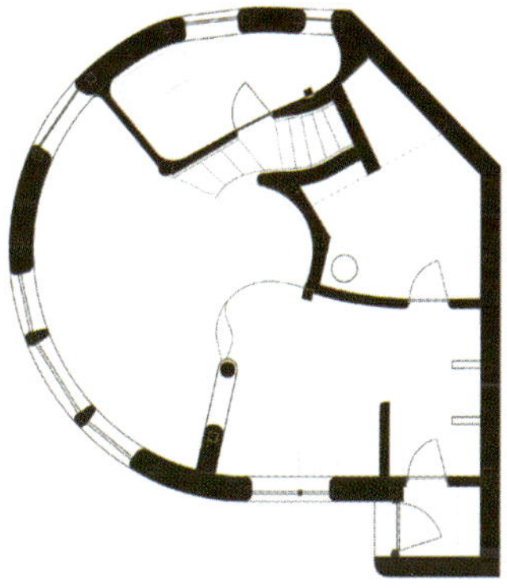

Ground floor plan

Studio Heya is an architecture and design studio founded by Nathalie Franquebalme in 2020 in Tokyo, and based in Mexico City since 2023.
Studio Heya questions, explores and designs regardless of being in different social, political and geographical contexts. It works between architecture, art and research, proposing schemes of collective creation. His work arises from observation and a multidisciplinary plastic process that helps the understanding of the site or object and gives input and guidance to the architecture and design. Studio Heya works on projects of different scales, from a Master plan, an architectural project, to furniture and object design.
Nathalie has collaborated with Alberto Kalach, Nikken Sekkei and Kengo Kuma & Associates.

Studio Heya ist ein Architektur- und Designstudio, das 2020 von Nathalie Franquebalme in Tokio gegründet wurde und seit 2023 in Mexiko-Stadt ansässig ist.
Das Studio Heya hinterfragt, erforscht und entwirft unabhängig von verschiedenen sozialen, politischen und geografischen Kontexten. Es arbeitet an der Schnittstelle zwischen Architektur, Kunst und Forschung und schlägt Schemata kollektiven Schaffens vor. Seine Arbeit entsteht aus der Beobachtung und einem multidisziplinären plastischen Prozess, der zum Verständnis des Ortes oder Objekts beiträgt und der Architektur und dem Design Input und Anleitung gibt. Das Studio Heya arbeitet an Projekten unterschiedlicher Größenordnung, von einem Masterplan über ein Architekturprojekt bis hin zu Möbel- und Objektdesign.
Nathalie hat mit Alberto Kalach, Nikken Sekkei und Kengo Kuma & Associates zusammengearbeitet.

Studio Heya est un studio d'architecture et de design fondé par Nathalie Franquebalme en 2020 à Tokyo, et basé à Mexico depuis 2023.
Studio Heya questionne, explore et conçoit indépendamment des contextes sociaux, politiques et géographiques différents. Il travaille entre l'architecture, l'art et la recherche, proposant des schémas de création collective. Son travail découle de l'observation et d'un processus plastique multidisciplinaire qui aide à la compréhension du site ou de l'objet et donne des informations et des orientations à l'architecture et au design. Studio Heya travaille sur des projets de différentes échelles, d'un plan directeur à un projet architectural, en passant par le design de meubles et d'objets.
Nathalie a collaboré avec Alberto Kalach, Nikken Sekkei et Kengo Kuma & Associates.

Studio Heya es un taller de arquitectura y diseño fundado por Nathalie Franquebalme en 2020 en la ciudad de Tokio, y con sede en Ciudad de México desde 2023.
Studio Heya cuestiona, explora y diseña sin importar encontrarse en diferentes contextos sociales, políticos y geográficos. Trabaja entre la arquitectura, el arte y la investigación planteando esquemas de creación colectiva. Su trabajo surge de la observación y de un proceso multidisciplinario plástico que ayuda al entendimiento del sitio u objeto y dan entrada y pauta a la arquitectura y al diseño. Studio Heya trabaja en proyectos de diferentes escalas, desde un Máster plan, un proyecto arquitectónico, hasta el diseño de mobiliario y de objetos.
Nathalie ha colaborado con Alberto Kalach, Nikken Sekkei y Kengo Kuma & Associates.

Studio Heya

www.studioheya.com

Nathalie Franquebalme

Casa Valle

Valle de Bravo, Mexico // Photos © Camila Cossio

Casa Valle is a harmonious fusion of renovation and architectural expansion, especially noticeable in the transformation of the old bay, built in the "Chalet" style.
The house features a main extension inspired by the Japanese "engawa" concept, characterised by two horizontal planes that facilitate a seamless connection between the interior and exterior. The raised floor and roof establish a tactile link with nature.
Wood was incorporated throughout the project, from the structure to the interior finishes and furniture design, fostering an atmosphere of warmth, serenity and a perfect balance between the modern and the classic. At Casa Valle, every detail was designed. We believe in the importance of craftsmanship, detail and landscape integration.

Casa Valle ist eine harmonische Verschmelzung von Renovierung und architektonischer Erweiterung, die sich besonders in der Umgestaltung des alten Erkers im Chalet-Stil zeigt. Das Haus verfügt über einen Hauptanbau, der vom japanischen „engawa"-Konzept inspiriert ist und sich durch zwei horizontale Ebenen auszeichnet, die eine nahtlose Verbindung zwischen Innen und Außen ermöglichen. Der Doppelboden und das Dach stellen eine taktile Verbindung zur Natur her. Holz wurde im gesamten Projekt verwendet, von der Struktur bis hin zu den Innenausstattungen und dem Möbeldesign, wodurch eine Atmosphäre der Wärme, der Gelassenheit und des perfekten Gleichgewichts zwischen Moderne und Klassik geschaffen wurde. Bei Casa Valle wurde jedes Detail geplant. Wir glauben an die Bedeutung von Handwerkskunst, Details und die Integration der Landschaft.

Casa Valle est une fusion harmonieuse de rénovation et d'agrandissement architectural, particulièrement perceptible dans la transformation de l'ancienne baie, construite dans le style « Chalet ». La maison présente une extension principale inspirée du concept japonais « engawa », caractérisée par deux plans horizontaux facilitant une connexion sans faille entre l'intérieur et l'extérieur. Le sol surélevé et le toit établissent un lien tactile avec la nature. Le bois a été incorporé dans tout le projet, de la structure aux finitions intérieures et au design des meubles, favorisant une atmosphère de chaleur, de sérénité et un équilibre parfait entre le moderne et le classique. À Casa Valle, chaque détail a été conçu. Nous croyons en l'importance de l'artisanat, du détail et de l'intégration paysagère.

Casa Valle es una fusión armoniosa de renovación y expansión arquitectónica, especialmente notoria en la transformación de la antigua crujía, construida en el estilo «Chalet». La casa presenta una extensión principal inspirada en el concepto japonés «engawa», caracterizada por dos planos horizontales que facilitan una conexión fluida entre el interior y el exterior. El suelo elevado y el techo establecen un vínculo táctil con la naturaleza.
La madera se incorporó en todo el proyecto, desde la estructura hasta los acabados interiores y el diseño del mobiliario, fomentando una atmósfera de calidez, serenidad y un equilibrio perfecto entre lo moderno y lo clásico.
En la Casa Valle, cada detalle fue diseñado. Creemos en la importancia de la artesanía, el detalle y la integración del paisaje.

Studio Onu's philosophy is to create designs with the potential to carry a narrative to the future. The practice learns from the past by reinventing forgotten artefacts, viewing traditions through a new lens and celebrating the history of former generations. It begins every design by learning about the client; their personality, background, passions, and dreams – this all has an impact, informing each proposal. The natural environment and regionally-sourced treasures of a project's location influence its design, and attention to these details forms a defining quality of Studio Onu's work. Architecture goes far beyond the physical walls.
Founded in 2020 by UK-trained architect Kuba Tomaszczyk, Studio Onu is an award-winning Basel-based practice, working internationally. Its current focus is on small scale rural projects in Poland, Switzerland and Denmark. Studio Onu has developed a reputation for modest and respectful designs that, despite small budgets, have gained international recognition.

Die Philosophie von Studio Onu ist es, Designs mit dem Potenzial zu schaffen, eine Erzählung in die Zukunft zu transportieren. Das Studio lernt aus der Vergangenheit, indem es vergessene Artefakte neu erfindet, Traditionen durch eine neue Linse betrachtet und die Geschichte früherer Generationen feiert. Es beginnt jedes Design, indem es den Kunden kennenlernt: ihre Persönlichkeit, Hintergründe, Leidenschaften und Träume, die alle eine Auswirkung haben und jeden Vorschlag informieren. Die natürliche Umgebung und die regionalen Schätze des Standorts eines Projekts beeinflussen sein Design, und die Aufmerksamkeit für diese Details bildet eine bestimmende Qualität der Arbeit von Studio Onu.
Architektur geht weit über physische Wände hinaus. 2020 von dem in Großbritannien ausgebildeten Architekten Kuba Tomaszczyk gegründet, ist Studio Onu ein preisgekröntes Büro mit Sitz in Basel, das international arbeitet. Sein aktueller Fokus liegt auf ländlichen Kleinskalaprojekten in Polen, der Schweiz und Dänemark. Studio Onu hat sich einen Ruf für bescheidene und respektvolle Designs erarbeitet, die trotz begrenzter Budgets international anerkannt wurden.

La philosophie de Studio Onu est de créer des designs avec le potentiel de transmettre une narration vers l'avenir. Le studio apprend du passé en réinventant des artefacts oubliés, en observant les traditions à travers un nouveau prisme et en célébrant l'histoire des générations précédentes. Il commence chaque conception en apprenant sur le client ; sa personnalité, son parcours, ses passions et ses rêves, tout cela ayant un impact et influençant chaque proposition. L'environnement naturel et les trésors d'origine régionale de l'emplacement d'un projet influent sur sa conception, et l'attention portée à ces détails forme une qualité déterminante du travail de Studio Onu. L'architecture va bien au-delà des murs physiques.
Fondé en 2020 par l'architecte formé au Royaume-Uni Kuba Tomaszczyk, Studio Onu est un cabinet basé à Bâle, primé et travaillant à l'international. Son focus actuel est sur des projets ruraux de petite échelle en Pologne, en Suisse et au Danemark. Studio Onu s'est forgé une réputation pour des designs modestes et respectueux qui, malgré des budgets réduits, ont gagné une reconnaissance internationale.

La filosofía de Studio Onu es crear diseños con el potencial de transmitir una narrativa hacia el futuro. El estudio aprende del pasado reinventando artefactos olvidados, observando tradiciones a través de una nueva lente y celebrando la historia de generaciones anteriores. Comienza cada diseño aprendiendo sobre el cliente; su personalidad, antecedentes, pasiones y sueños, todo esto tiene un impacto e informa cada propuesta. El entorno natural y los tesoros de origen regional de la ubicación de un proyecto influyen en su diseño, y la atención a estos detalles forma una cualidad definitoria del trabajo de Studio Onu. La arquitectura va mucho más allá de las paredes físicas.
Fundada en 2020 por el arquitecto entrenado en el Reino Unido Kuba Tomaszczyk, Studio Onu es un despacho con sede en Basilea, galardonado y que trabaja internacionalmente. Su enfoque actual se centra en proyectos rurales de pequeña escala en Polonia, Suiza y Dinamarca. Studio Onu ha desarrollado una reputación por diseños modestos y respetuosos que, a pesar de los presupuestos reducidos, han ganado reconocimiento internacional.

Studio Onu

www.onusudio.com

Kuba Tomaszczyk

Dom Las

DOM LAS ("Forest House" in Polish) is a project born from a specific situation. 25 years ago, the client bought an empty field near his hometown, with the vision to create something for the future. Through care and attention, the 7 hectares have been transformed into an attractive and varied landscape, reflecting the native flora of the region. The buildings are a result of a conversation between the vernacular style of Poland's Kashubia region, the traditional materials of the area and the natural environment. Although the brief was minimal, the building needed to serve two different but complimentary functions: to enable the continued care of the land, but also offer occasional shelter for the client and his family. The result is two buildings which have a relationship to each other, but also to the landscape in which they are placed. This is emphasized through the materials used and details incorporated, the craftsmanship of local skilled workers, and the celebration of family heirlooms.

DOM LAS („Waldhaus" auf Polnisch) ist ein Projekt, das vor 25 Jahren entstand. Der Bauherr kaufte ein Feld in der Nähe seiner Heimatstadt mit der Vision, etwas für die Zukunft zu schaffen. Durch Sorgfalt und Aufmerksamkeit wurden die 7 Hektar in eine attraktive und vielfältige Landschaft verwandelt, die die einheimische Flora der Region widerspiegelt. Die Gebäude sind das Ergebnis eines Dialogs zwischen dem volkstümlichen Stil der Region Kaschubei in Polen und den traditionellen Materialien. Obwohl die Anweisungen minimal waren, musste das Gebäude zwei verschiedene, aber ergänzende Funktionen erfüllen: die kontinuierliche Pflege des Geländes ermöglichen, aber auch gelegentlich Schutz für den Kunden und seine Familie bieten. Das Ergebnis sind zwei Gebäude, die sowohl miteinander als auch mit der Landschaft, in der sie sich befinden, in Beziehung stehen. Dies wird durch die verwendeten Materialien und die eingebauten Details, das Handwerk lokaler spezialisierter Arbeiter und die Feier von Familienerbstücken betont.

DOM LAS (« Maison de la Forêt » en polonais) est un projet né d'une situation spécifique. Il y a 25 ans, le client a acheté un champ vide près de sa ville natale, avec la vision de créer quelque chose pour l'avenir. Grâce au soin et à l'attention, les 7 hectares se sont transformés en un paysage attrayant et varié reflétant la flore native de la région. Les bâtiments sont le résultat d'une conversation entre le style vernaculaire de la région de Cachoubie en Pologne et les matériaux traditionnels.
Bien que les instructions fussent minimales, le bâtiment devait remplir deux fonctions différentes mais complémentaires : permettre l'entretien continu du terrain, mais aussi offrir un abri occasionnel au client et à sa famille. Le résultat sont deux bâtiments qui ont une relation entre eux, mais aussi avec le paysage dans lequel ils sont situés. Cela est souligné à travers les matériaux utilisés et les détails incorporés, l'artisanat de travailleurs locaux spécialisés et la célébration des reliques familiales.

DOM LAS («Casa del Bosque» en polaco) es un proyecto nacido de una situación especifica. Hace 25 años, el cliente compró un campo vacio cerca de su ciudad natal, con la visión de crear algo para el futuro. A través del cuidado y la atención, las 7 ha. se han transformado en un paisaje atractivo y variado que refleja la flora nativa de la región. Los edificios son el resultado de una conversación entre el estilo vernáculo de la región de Kashubia de Polonia y los materiales tradicionales. Aunque las instrucciones fueron minimas, el edificio necesitaba cumplir dos funciones diferentes pero complementarias: permitir el cuidado continuo del terreno, pero también ofrecer refugio ocasional para el cliente y su familia. El resultado son dos edificios que tienen una relación entre sí, pero también con el paisaje en el que están ubicados. Esto se enfatiza a través de los materiales utilizados y los detalles incorporados, la artesanía de trabajadores locales especializados y la celebración de reliquias familiares.

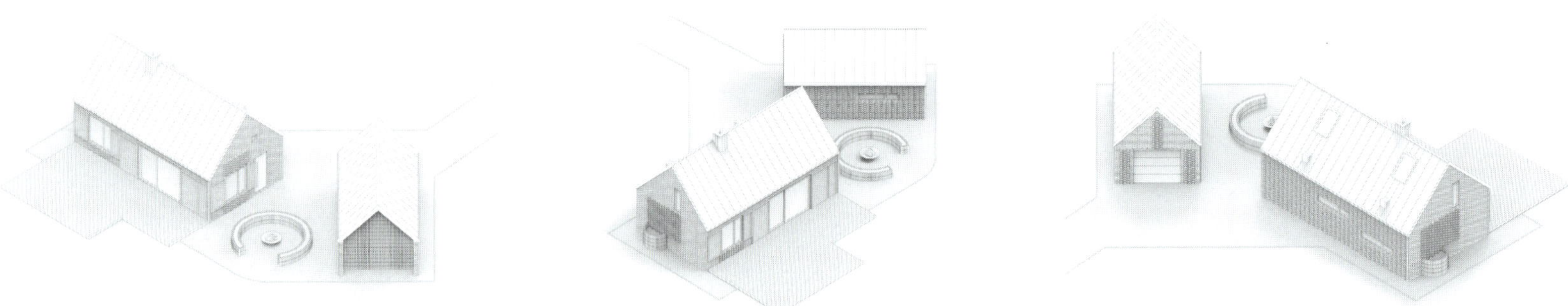

Axonometric views

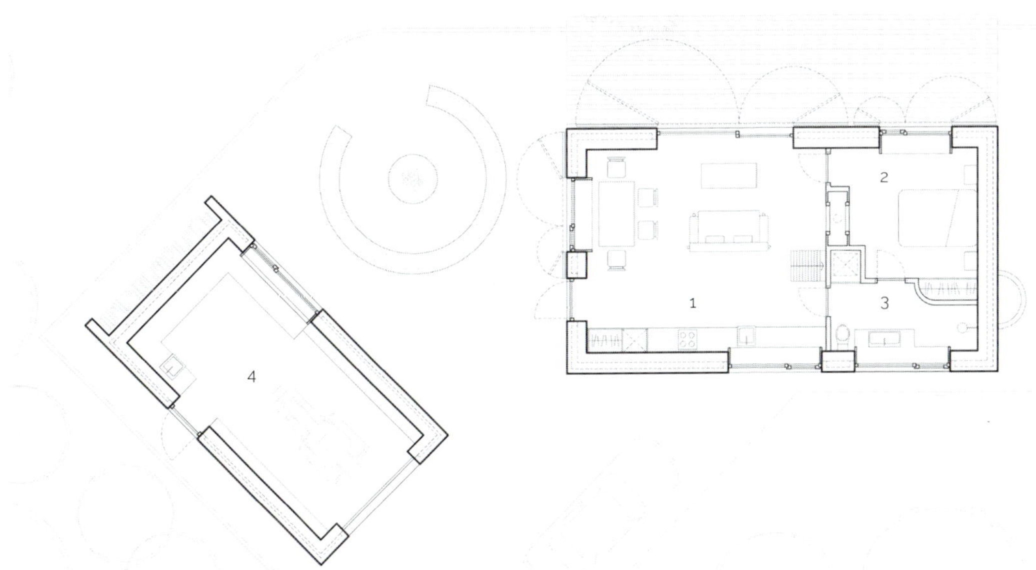

1. Living and dinning room, Kitchen
2. Bedroom
3. Bathroom
4. Agricultural workshop

Floor plan

Established in 2014 by Hideo Kimura and Junko Kimura in Kyoto, Japan, STUDIO RAKKORA ARCHITECTS embodies a commitment to architectural simplicity in materials, structure, and space. Our philosophy emphasizes a meticulous devotion to detail, whereby each element is delicately considered to express a sense of inevitability.
Central to our architectural ethos is the evolving character of natural materials with the passage of time, which fosters a sense of continuity within space. This commitment, rooted in principles of locality and sustainability, guides our pursuit in forging vibrant environments through the seamless connection of time and space. We aim to cultivate dynamic atmospheres where people can experience its richness, thereby positively influencing both the immediate surroundings and the broader architectural context..

Gegründet im Jahr 2014 von Hideo Kimura und Junko Kimura in Kyoto, Japan, verkörpert STUDIO RAKKORA ARCHITECTS ein Engagement für architektonische Einfachheit in Materialien, Struktur und Raum. Unsere Philosophie betont eine sorgfältige Hingabe zum Detail, bei der jedes Element mit Zartheit betrachtet wird, um ein Gefühl der Unvermeidlichkeit auszudrücken.
Ein zentrales Element unserer architektonischen Ethik ist der evolutionäre Charakter natürlicher Materialien im Laufe der Zeit, der ein Gefühl der Kontinuität im Raum fördert. Dieses Engagement, verwurzelt in den Prinzipien der Lokalität und Nachhaltigkeit, leitet unsere Bemühungen, lebendige Umgebungen durch die nahtlose Verbindung von Zeit und Raum zu schaffen. Unser Ziel ist es, dynamische Atmosphären zu kultivieren, in denen Menschen ihren Reichtum erleben können und damit sowohl die unmittelbare Umgebung als auch den größeren architektonischen Kontext positiv beeinflussen.

Fondé en 2014 par Hideo Kimura et Junko Kimura à Kyoto, au Japon, STUDIO RAKKORA ARCHITECTS incarne un engagement envers la simplicité architecturale en termes de matériaux, de structure et d'espace. Notre philosophie met l'accent sur un dévouement méticuleux au détail, où chaque élément est considéré avec délicatesse pour exprimer une sensation d'inévitabilité.
Un élément central de notre éthique architecturale est le caractère évolutif des matériaux naturels avec le temps, qui favorise une sensation de continuité dans l'espace. Cet engagement, enraciné dans les principes de localité et de durabilité, guide notre effort pour forger des environnements dynamiques à travers la connexion fluide du temps et de l'espace. Notre objectif est de cultiver des atmosphères dynamiques dans lesquelles les gens peuvent expérimenter leur richesse, influençant ainsi positivement à la fois l'environnement immédiat et le contexte architectural plus large.

Establecido en 2014 por Hideo Kimura y Junko Kimura en Kioto, Japón, STUDIO RAKKORA ARCHITECTS encarna un compromiso con la simplicidad arquitectónica en materiales, estructura y espacio. Nuestra filosofia hace hincapié en una meticulosa devoción por el detalle, en la que cada elemento se considera con delicadeza para expresar una sensación de inevitabilidad.
Un elemento central de nuestra ética arquitectónica es el carácter evolutivo de los materiales naturales con el paso del tiempo, que fomenta una sensación de continuidad en el espacio. Este compromiso, arraigado en los principios de localidad y sostenibilidad, guia nuestro empeño por forjar entornos vibrantes a través de la conexión fluida del tiempo y el espacio. Nuestro objetivo es cultivar atmósferas dinámicas en las que las personas puedan experimentar su riqueza, influyendo asi positivamente tanto en el entorno inmediato como en el contexto arquitectónico más amplio.

Studio Rakkora Architects

www.studiorakkora.com

Junko Kimura
Hideo Kimura

House in Hanno

Small Building

Hanno, Japan // Photos © Tetsuya Hayashiguchi

Nestled in Okumusashi, the Hanno house is made from local timber and seamlessly integrates with the village's natural splendor. The layout was planned to draw the surrounding trees and local landscape into the house. Approaching from the West, the house unfolds along a farm road, with its layout extending the path into the dwelling. Inside, a lengthy earthen floor space mirrors this road, serving as a living conduit that traverses the central axis of the architecture.
Along this earthen floor, three alternately stacked volumes interconnect, allowing light and air to permeate the entire space. The structure anticipates a diversity of living experiences by enabling the residents to immerse themselves within the landscape and the everyday scenes unfolding within its envelope.

Eingebettet in Okumusashi, ist das Hanno-Haus aus heimischem Holz gebaut und integriert sich perfekt in die natürliche Pracht des Dorfes. Die Aufteilung wurde so geplant, dass die umliegenden Bäume und die lokale Landschaft in das Haus integriert werden. Wenn man sich von Westen nähert, erstreckt sich das Haus entlang eines landwirtschaftlichen Weges, und sein Grundriss verlängert den Weg zum Wohnhaus. Im Inneren reflektiert ein langer Erdgeschossboden den Weg und dient als lebenswichtiger Kanal, der die zentrale Achse der Architektur durchquert. Entlang dieses Erdgeschossbodens sind drei abwechselnd gestapelte Volumina miteinander verbunden, wodurch Licht und Luft den gesamten Raum durchdringen können. Die Struktur antizipiert eine Vielfalt lebenswichtiger Erfahrungen, indem sie es den Bewohnern ermöglicht, in die Landschaft und die alltäglichen Szenen einzutauchen, die sich innerhalb ihrer Hülle abspielen.

Nichée à Okumusashi, la maison Hanno est construite avec du bois local et s'intègre parfaitement dans la splendeur naturelle du village. La disposition a été planifiée de manière à ce que les arbres environnants et le paysage local soient intégrés dans la maison. En approchant depuis l'ouest, la maison s'étend le long d'un chemin agricole, et son agencement prolonge le chemin vers le logement. À l'intérieur, un long sol de terre reflète le chemin et sert de conduit vital traversant l'axe central de l'architecture. Tout au long de ce sol de terre, trois volumes empilés alternativement s'interconnectent, permettant à la lumière et à l'air d'imprégner tout l'espace. La structure anticipe une diversité d'expériences vitales en permettant aux résidents de se plonger dans le paysage et dans les scènes quotidiennes qui se déroulent dans leur enveloppe.

Enclavada en Okumusashi, la casa Hanno está construida con madera local y se integra perfectamente en el esplendor natural del pueblo. La distribución se planificó de forma que los árboles de los alrededores y el paisaje local se integraran en la casa. Al acercarse desde el oeste, la casa se despliega a lo largo de un camino agrícola, y su trazado prolonga el camino hacia la vivienda. En el interior, un largo suelo de tierra refleja el camino y sirve de conducto vital que atraviesa el eje central de la arquitectura.
A lo largo de este suelo de tierra, tres volúmenes apilados alternativamente se interconectan, permitiendo que la luz y el aire impregnen todo el espacio. La estructura anticipa una diversidad de experiencias vitales al permitir a los residentes sumergirse en el paisaje y en las escenas cotidianas que se desarrollan dentro de su envoltura.

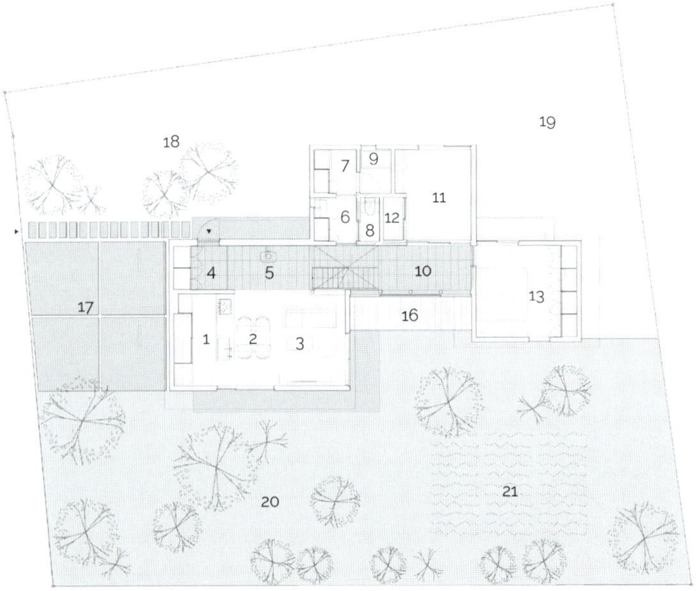

First floor plan

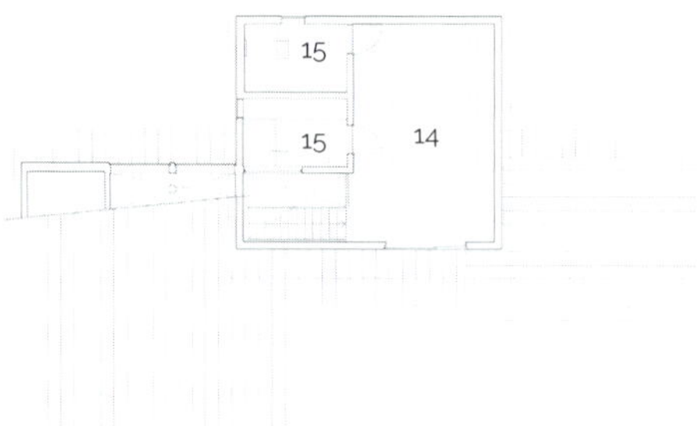

Second floor plan

1. Kitchen
2. Dining
3. Living
4. Entrance
5. Hole
6. Washroom
7. Dressing room
8. WC
9. Bathroom
10. Earthern floor
11. Japanese style room
12. Closet
13. Bed room
14. Refresh room
15. Study room
16. Terrace
17. Parking
18. Front yard
19. Backyard
20. Orchard
21. Field

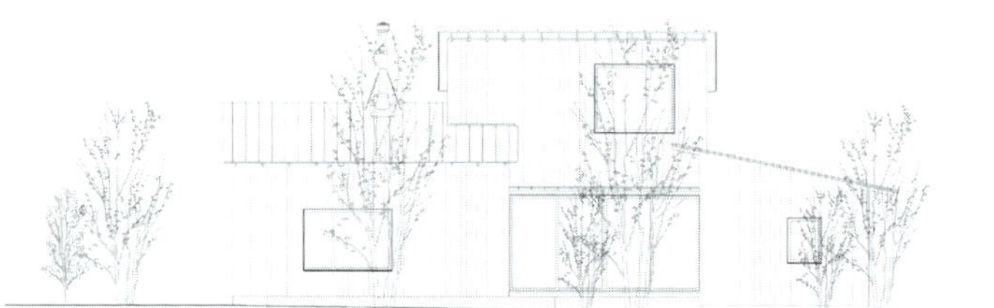

Southern elevation

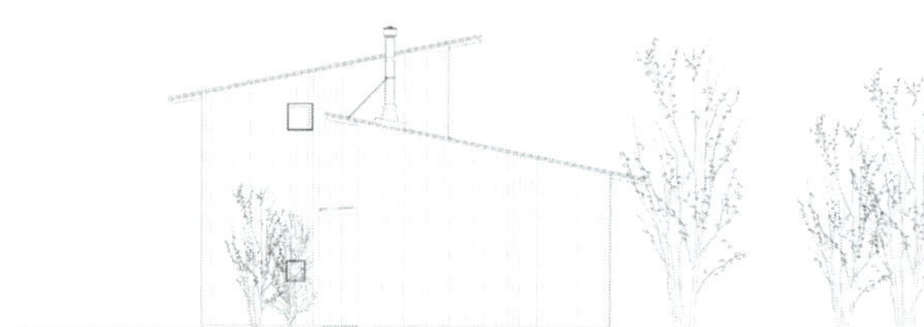

Western elevation

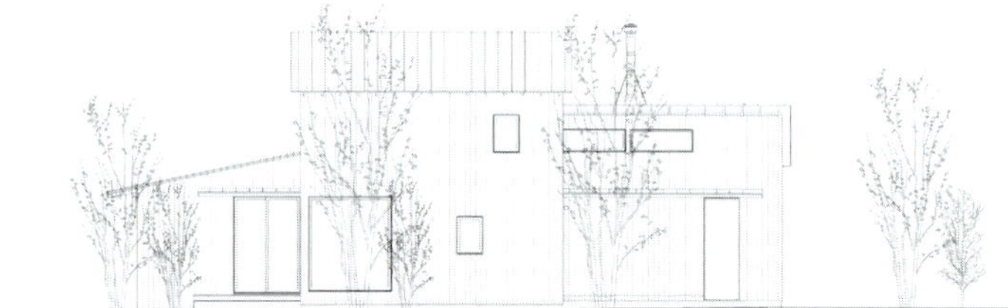

Northern elevation

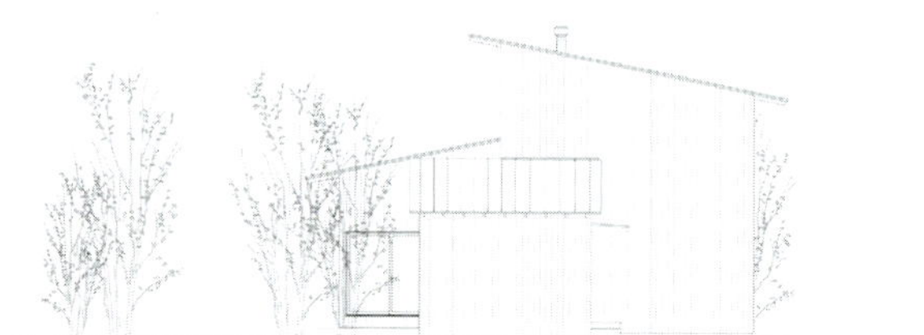

Eastern elevation

Kyoto, Japan // Photos © Tetsuya Hayashiguchi

Situated in Kyoto City's residential area, this narrow 4-story RC building defies conventional structural norms. Instead of adhering to a typical RC wall configuration, our design approach involves sculpting a concrete mass based on site conditions, intricately carving space from within. The juxtaposition of limited space and expansive openings fosters unity with the surroundings, transforming the building's narrowness into a distinctive allure. We harmonize materials, details, and scale, erasing hierarchical relationships among elements like interior materials, furniture, and equipment against the fair-faced concrete structure. This yields a sense of transparency within the composition — a dance between visible and unseen elements akin to the thoughtful intervals and pauses within the space.

In einem Wohnviertel von Kyoto gelegen, trotzt dieses schmale vierstöckige Gebäude den herkömmlichen strukturellen Normen. Anstatt sich an die typische Konfiguration von CR-Wänden zu halten, besteht unser Designansatz darin, eine Masse aus Beton entsprechend den örtlichen Bedingungen zu modellieren und den Raum von innen heraus kunstvoll zu gestalten. Die Kombination von begrenztem Raum und großen Öffnungen fördert die Einheit mit der Umgebung und verwandelt die Enge des Gebäudes in ein markantes Merkmal. Wir harmonisieren Materialien, Details und Maßstab, indem wir hierarchische Beziehungen zwischen Elementen wie Innenmaterialien, Möbeln und Ausstattung gegenüber der Sichtbetonstruktur verwischen, was eine Transparenz in der Komposition, einen Tanz zwischen sichtbaren und unsichtbaren Elementen, ähnlich den Intervallen und Pausen, die im Raum auftreten.

Situé dans la zone résidentielle de Kyoto, ce bâtiment étroit de quatre étages défie les normes structurelles conventionnelles. Au lieu de suivre la configuration typique des murs de CR, notre approche de conception consiste à sculpter une masse de béton en fonction des conditions du site, sculptant de manière complexe l'espace de l'intérieur. La juxtaposition de l'espace limité et des grandes ouvertures favorise l'unité avec l'environnement, transformant l'étroitesse du bâtiment en un élément distinctif attrayant. Nous harmonisons les matériaux, les détails et l'échelle, effaçant les relations hiérarchiques entre les éléments tels que les matériaux intérieurs, les meubles et l'équipement par rapport à la structure en béton apparent, produisant une sensation de transparence dans la composition, une danse entre les éléments visibles et invisibles similaire aux intervalles et pauses qui se produisent dans l'espace.

Situado en la zona residencial de Kioto, este estrecho edificio de cuatro plantas desafía las normas estructurales convencionales. En lugar de ceñirnos a la típica configuración de muros de CR, nuestro planteamiento de diseño consiste en esculpir una masa de hormigón en función de las condiciones del lugar, tallando intrincadamente el espacio desde dentro. La yuxtaposición de espacio limitado y grandes aberturas fomenta la unidad con el entorno, transformando la estrechez del edificio en un atractivo distintivo. Armonizamos materiales, detalles y escala, borrando las relaciones jerárquicas entre elementos como los materiales interiores, el mobiliario y el equipamiento frente a la estructura de hormigón visto, produciendo una sensación de transparencia en la composición, una danza entre elementos visibles e invisibles similar a los intervalos y pausas que se producen en el espacio.

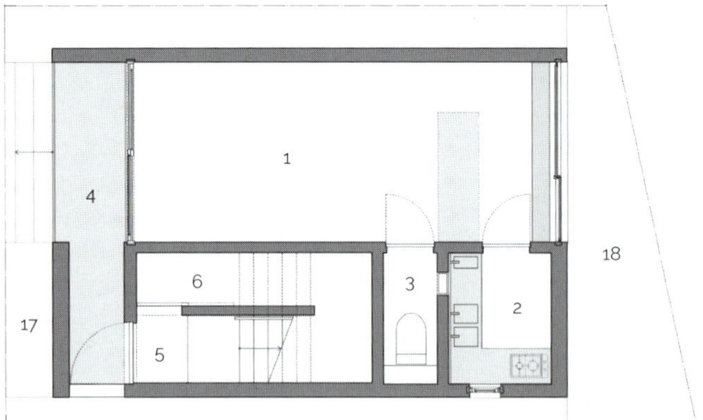

First floor plan

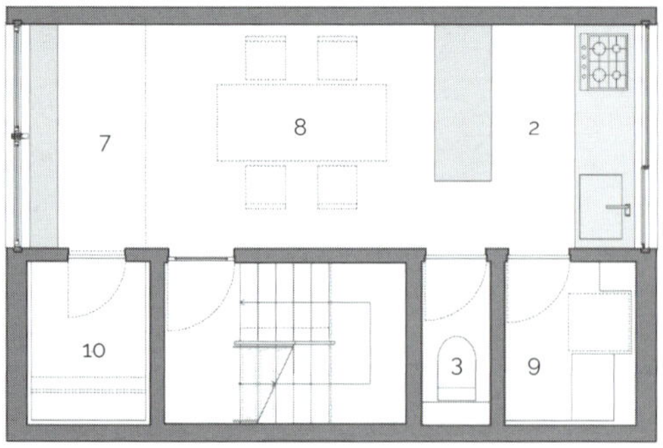

Second floor plan

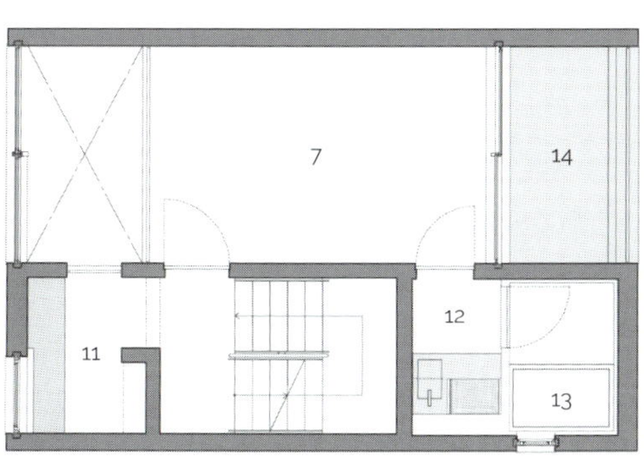

Third floor plan

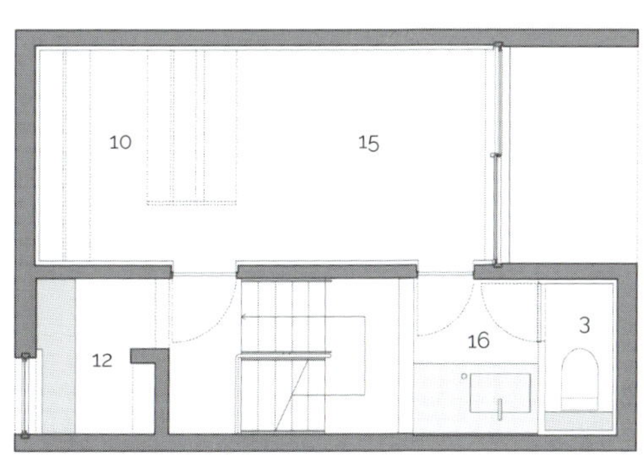

Fourth floor plan

1. Office/Shop
2. Kitchen
3. WC
4. Approach
5. Entrance
6. Storage
7. Living
8. Dining
9. Pantry
10. WIC
11. Study room
12. Dressing/ laundry room
13. Bathroom
14. Balcony
15. Attic
16. Washroom
17. Front yard
18. Garden